Thomas, I pray these words touch you

DOC

KEPT
by
Edward "Doc" Amey

KEPT

Credits and acknowledgements:

Cover images: Kevin Herrin

Sal Chapa image: Kevin Woods

Jack Roady image: Chris Bell

Editing: Eloise Herrin and Robin McCardell

Court Documents: Galveston County Court House

Fellowship Bible Certificates: Fellowship Bible College

Finding God in a Pig Sty article:"This article orginally appeared in Crossroad Extra, a newsletter for Crossroad Bible Institute. Crossroad is an international prison ministry. Its mission is to mobilize and equip the church to be in life-changing relationships with prisoners all over the world. More information can be found at www.crossroadbible.org.

Scripture taken from the New King James Version®. Copyright © 1982 by Thomas Nelson. Used by permission. All rights reserved

copyright © 2016 Edward "Doc" Amey

All rights reserved.

ISBN-13:
978-1533598691

ISBN-10:
153359869X

DEDICATIONS

My first dedication would have to be to Jesus Christ, my Lord and Savior, for getting on the Cross and paying a debt that He didn't owe. Without Him I wouldn't be able to write my story of redemption.

The next dedication would be to my Grandmother, Elnora Linville, who I know is smiling down from Heaven watching over me and witnessing all her prayers on my behalf being answered. "RIP Grandma until we meet again."

Another RIP to my Father, Lawrence Edward Davis, who was murdered when I was 6 months old, but without him there is no me. So "Until we meet again Pops, I love you."

A special dedication to my beautiful mother, Wanda Ball, who had to put up with me and all my mischief from the time I was 3. We get to look back on it now and laugh about a bunch of things that at one time brought her many tears. So "Thank you Mama, I love you very much."

I also want to dedicate this book to my children, Edward Jr., Morgan, Lawryn, and Brenden. I may not have been the best Father when you were growing up, and for that I am very sorry.

To my brother Dominique. I know we have had some bumpy roads in life. I'm thanking God that those days are over and I want you to know I love you more than you can imagine.

To my baby sister, Lenora who has grown into a beautiful woman. I love you more than you will ever know as well.

To my Uncle Greg, I love you, and thank you for all the tough love that you gave me.

To Aunt Ann, Thank you for all the prayers, tough love, and discipline you gave me throughout my life. For that I will be forever be indebted. I truly thank you and love you very much.

To My cousin/brother, Cornelius Jackson, AKA Mr. C. Words could never express the bond we share, so I'm not going to even try. You know what it is and I thank you for everything bro. What's understood needs no explanation.

To my cousin Tasha and the Corpus Clan, I love you guys very much.

This portion I will dedicate to my spiritual family that God has put in to my life to guide, lead, and teach me the things about Him.

My first dedication is to my Spiritual Father, Terry Melancon, who God lined me up with and has discipled me into the man God intended for me to be. At the beginning, I was very rough around the edges, but he endured and had patience with me. For that, I thank God for you.

My Spiritual Mama, Gina Estey. Thank you for seeing something in me that I didn't see or feel, but you did. Thank you for teaching me how to have the heart of a servant and the mind of a king and to serve with excellence. For that I will be forever grateful.

Bishop Delbert Herrin, and Mama Eloise, I can't find the words to describe the genuine love and encouraging words and just the monumental roles you have played in my life. I love you guys dearly.

To my pastors, Kevin and Melissa Herrin, I love you guys very much. Pastor Kevin, thank you for everything: the love, the correction, and the encouragement. Thank you very much for just being a real, genuine, solid man of God.

Thank you very much to my brothers Tre Hernandez and Robbie Fuentes. I love y'all bro. Thank you for the accountability that we hold each other to, the encouragement we give one another, and I just thank God for y'all.

To my Fellowship Church Family, its too many to name and if I tried I wouldn't want to leave anyone out—so you know who you are. I love you guys.

Last, but definitely not least, I want to dedicate this book to YOU—the reader. Thank you for taking time out of your busy schedule to read my personal testimony. I pray that it encourages you, in one way or another. I love you guys, and if you know someone who needs to hear my story, please put this in their hands. Thank you, and God bless you all.

~D.O.C~
AKA—**Disciple of Christ**

CONTENTS

Chapter One	1	Chapter Thirteen	37
Chapter Two	5	Chapter Fourteen	41
Chapter Three	7	Chapter Fifteen	47
Chapter Four	9	Chapter Sixteen	61
Chapter Five	11	Chapter Seventeen	65
Chapter Six	13	Chapter Eighteen	71
Chapter Seven	15	Chapter Nineteen	79
Chapter Eight	19	Chapter Twenty	81
Chapter Nine	21	Chapter Twenty-one	85
Chapter Ten	27	Chapter Twenty-two	89
Chapter eleven	31		
Chapter Twelve	33		

ACKNOWLEDGMENTS

I would like to take this time to acknowledge some people who have put time and effort into putting this project in to a reality.

I want to acknowledge God for keeping me through all of this and giving me the strength to live to tell about it and give Him the glory.

Dr, Luke Holter, who prophesied over me to write this book. I have thought about writing my testimony, but never really did it. When he gave me that word from God, I knew I had to do it.

Ms. Eloise Herrin, who is a spiritual mother. When I gave her this book it was 60 pages of one long complete thought. There was no punctuation anywhere, and she went through and shaped my story.

Robin McCardell, aka "Mini Monk", who took what Ms. Herrin had done and used her English skills to fix the flow of my story. I thank her very much for that.

Tammy McDonald, my sister in Christ and my Bible College classmate (as well as author of two amazing books, Shifted Vision and Conquering the Grief that Stole Christmas) who invited me into her home and helped me put the last pieces of this book together.

Pastor Kevin Herrin, of The Fellowship of Texas City, for taking the photos for the cover and back page.

Last, but not least, I want to acknowledge everyone who has supported this project whether it was through finances, time, prayer, or wisdom. It is greatly appreciated and may God bless you for your role in helping others learn to see how God has kept them.

Introduction

From DOC "Department of Corrections" to DOC "Disciple of Christ"

Of all the places I thought I would end up, this was not one of them. I was in the front row at the Fellowship of Texas City during morning service. When the praise team started singing, I was overwhelmed. As they sang about overcoming the world through Jesus, I thought about my life and all that I had overcome by the grace of God, gratitude fill my heart as I lifted my hands, and the tears streamed down my face I sang, "We have overcome, by the blood of the lamb and the word of our testimony." The place where I was standing seemed so far away from where my story began. Here's the story of how God kept me----I pray thru reading this you could look back on your life to see where God has kept you.

Section 1
THE WORLD I CAME FROM…A PRODUCT OF THE PROJECT

CHAPTER 1

LIFE IN THE GALVESTON PROJECTS

My name is Edward Demond Amey, AKA "Doc" Amey. I was born to Wanda Gail Amey and Lawrence Edward Davis on Feb 9, 1980 in Galveston, Texas at 4:42 PM. My father was killed in cold blood on the streets of Galveston on Oct. 18, 1980. I'm the middle child of 3 on my mother's side. My brother is four years older than I am and my sister is four years younger. On my father's side I am the baby of three brothers.

According to my mother, she and my Aunt Ann began smoking weed before I was born in 1980, then she began taking "downers" and drinking codeine syrup to add to smoking weed. My little sister was born in 1984, and by 1985 my mother was introduced to crack cocaine.

I can remember living in the projects of Galveston in Cedar Terrace with my mom, my little sister, and my sister's father. We lived in 44E. My Aunt Ann, Cornelius Jackson, who is my favorite cousin/brother in the world still to this day, his sister Tasha Jackson Corpus all lived there next door. We called Cornelius "Mr. C" and his sister we called "The Kid."

I also recall not having much to eat in those days, so we always ate buttered rice and sugar and a lot of syrup sandwiches. My older brother lived in Texas City with my grandmother. As a kid, I was often barred from my mother's room because she and my aunt were getting high. One night when we were living in Galveston, I walked into my mother's room. This guy walked out and she was smoking crack and she held the crack pipe up, still smoking, and told me "You see this?" "Don't ever mess with this because all it takes is one hit! Do you hear me?" I just looked at her because that was not my mother. Shortly after I went back in my room and just cried. Later, once I was a grown man, I told my mother about that incident and she didn't remember it. That came as no surprise. I figured she wouldn't.

When we were living in Galveston, kids talked about my clothes and how they stank. I didn't have top of the line clothes and my mother didn't always make us take baths. I went to school many days without bathing.

Speaking of baths, one day my cousin Mr. C and I had just come from church I think, because I still had on some black church socks. His room was directly across from the bathroom, so we would run from his room, jump in the tub, then run back, and jump into his bed. We must have been doing that for an hour while our mothers were in their room getting high. I can remember jumping off his bed, running to the tub, pushing myself off the wall, and running back full speed. As I started to jump, I slipped and my momentum took me head first into the corner of my cousin's bed. I hit the bottom of my left eye socket. My cousin was yelling, "His eye is coming out!" over and over really loud! He was running to his mom's room trying to get her attention. I was five or six years old, and hearing that my eye was falling out caused me to burst into tears. Our mothers were so high they never thought of calling an ambulance or 911. I didn't get any medical attention that night. My cousins' mom, my Aunt Ann, was shaking uncontrollably while she put a sock on my face to stop the bleeding and almost drowned me with peroxide.

THE BURNING COUCH

As time went on, I remember my Aunt Janice on Dad's side staying with us for a while because she and her children's father, Zay had gotten into a fight. She was sleeping on our couch. The way the project apartments were built, the mailbox was a slot in the wall just over the couch in the living room. One night, when everyone was sleeping, Aunt Janice's boyfriend threw a towel soaked in gasoline through the mail slot. He set the couch on fire. We rushed out of the apartment. Two weeks later, my sister's dad caught Aunt Janice's boyfriend in front of the liquor store across the street from the projects and beat him with a wooden club. I witnessed the whole thing. From a young age I can remember seeing lots of fights and getting into many fights myself. This was just one of many sights I saw growing up in the projects

CHAPTER 2

LIFE AT GRANDMA'S

One day, my Uncle Freddy and my brother came to pick me up and moved me to Texas City to live with my grandma. She was a God-fearing woman who lived in Mae's Apts on 5th Ave. There were about six of us living in the apartment. I was the baby, so I was in heaven. I got really spoiled. As a matter of fact, on my sixth birthday, she took me to Toys 'R Us and let us "ball till we fall baby." She bought me pretty much whatever I wanted. One time, in 1988, it snowed in Texas City and Grandma let us stay home from school to play in the snow. Ah, those were the good times.

When I was around 9 years old, we moved to 5th Avenue in the Chelsea district of Texas City. In that neighborhood things were not great. My mom, while trying to rehabilitate herself, moved in with us (my brother, my little sister and two uncles) in my grandma's house. My mom would try to discipline me for things she saw me getting into, but I would run to my grandma for sympathy. In her eyes I could do no wrong. My mom ended up leaving and started using drugs again. Which continued off and on for many years.

THE CHURCH THAT TOUCHED MY YOUNG LIFE

By 1990-91 my mom got cleaned up again, and got her own place on the corner of 4th Avenue and 11th Street. My brother and I moved in with her. Our neighbors, the Rawls, Kendrick, Everick, Staffany and Tiffany would end up playing an important part of my life. I was between 10 and 11 years old at the time. a white man named Bud Brown (we called him Brother Bud) would come every Sunday morning faithfully and pick me and my sister and the Rawls kids up for Sunday School at Christ Temple on 29th St N. I remember Brother Bud letting everyone in the bus, but when I would get in, he would grab me by the ear and twist it a bit before asking me if I was going to be good in church. I would nod my head yeah and he would let me go. I really loved going to that church. That was where I first received my first real revelation of God and Jesus, His son. My children's pastor was named Brother Kevin Herrin and he always gave me big hugs and candy. I loved those people at that church. The things I learned there kept me. Even though I got away and it was several years before I made it back, the moments there created something like a compass point for me.

CHAPTER 3

CULTURE OF DRUGS AND CRIME

Around the time I was twelve years old, I became a product of my environment. My brother is 15-16 years old now and that's when I started hanging out with my cousin Daniel. Daniel's daddy was one of the biggest drug dealers in town at the time. When people saw Daniel and me coming, they already knew it was trouble. Believe it or not, I thought I was bad, but no, this dude was bad and he was two years younger than I was. His whole family was notorious for selling drugs and living a life of crime all the way from his grandmother down to his youngest brother. His dad, William, was the gangster of gangsters. He even used to beat up cops.

My cousin Jeremiah got shot in the face by this girl. While he was waiting for the ambulance, the girl's family was in the process of moving out of the house. They lived in fear that Daniel's dad and his posse would do something to them. Boy, were they right! The next morning their whole house was burned to the ground. That was just one of the many incidents.

Daniel and I formed a very tight bond because of all the things that happened. When you saw him you saw me and when you saw me, he was there, too. We were like brothers and I even called his dad my dad. I began to get the same privileges Daniel got. We started to drop off drugs and get paid for it by his father.

Then one day the police were doing a sting operation. I

saw a car leave the police station and it parked on the corner by my house. The policeman, dressed in plain clothes, let a man out to walk to Daniel's house and buy drugs from his dad. I saw this happen three times, so I ran over there to tell them what I saw. Nobody believed me but my Uncle Joe who immediately left. Then Daniel and I, his brother, Jeremiah, and another cousin, Shawn, all took off on our bikes hurrying toward the police station. I wanted to show them the car that had been leaving from the station and dropping off a man a block away from their house to buy drugs. We made it three houses down the block from Daniel's house when we saw about six vans with a task force or swat team. When we started to turn around and go they already had vans coming from the other end of the street to block it off. It was like everything moved in slow motion until suddenly we heard gunshots, screeching tires, and saw arrests being made. They were busted! We went into the house after they left and they had demolished it. They knocked holes in the wall, busted open cereal boxes, and left nothing unturned. It was a total disaster. From that day forward I had a hatred for cops—not that I ever liked them, but after that day I really hated them all.

CHAPTER 4

THE G-RAGE AND THE WEED HOUSE

By 1992 I was 12 years old, smoking weed and "thugging" on a regular basis. I was trying to be sneaky about the weed and went to my grandma's house. She smelled it, of course, and I knew I was in trouble. She called me Edward, the only person in the whole world who used my first name. She said, "You been smokin' weed!" I tried to lie at first and deny it. She grabbed my hand and sniffed it and said, "Yes, you have, but if you gonna smoke weed at least do it in the house so you don't get in no trouble!"

My grandma always kept a stash of weed in a tin cookie can in the cabinet that me and my brother used to hit up all the time. When my brother was selling weed, he would send me to Grandma's house to get it for whoever he was selling to. One day about an ounce of it came up missing and my brother accused me of taking it. We argued and argued but about a week later I was hitting the tin can and there it was—the ounce of weed my brother was missing. My grandma had taken it and there was nothing he could do about it. She had been snooping in my brother's room and found his stash so she knew he was selling.

As time goes on, my grandmother was put into a nursing home. My brother and I move back to my mother's house on the corner of 4th Avenue and 11th Street next door to the Rawls. Instead of her being our parent, though, she is more like our friend. So we kinda ran loose—hustling and smoking weed. Our house was the neighborhood hangout. We had the "G-rage", the corner house right across the street from the grocery store. We had a basketball goal on our garage and that made it the spot to be. Anybody that hung out in Chelsea knew about the "G-rage".

A lot of things that the average 12 year old should never see at that age, I saw every day. Women were selling their bodies for drugs. People were getting beat because they owed for the drugs. Shooting dice, drinking, smoking weed, and all sorts of crimes were being done in that neighborhood.

CHAPTER 5

GANG BANGING IN THE CHELSEA—1993

I was 13 years old and gangs had gotten really bad in Galveston County. Certain neighborhoods had their particular gangs. The older dudes I looked up to were Crips, so I became a Crip. Crips wear blue. My brother was a Blood so we didn't mix too well, to say the least. Back in those days, the Bloods and the Crips were black gangs. Before anybody started choosing sides, there were some of them that grew up together. There was a Mexican gang called the Brown Assassins, B.A. for short. They didn't like blacks so that put them against the Bloods and the Crips. My gang-banging days were more about blacks against Mexicans, B.A. to be specific. It was crazy! There were days when we couldn't walk through the train park or anywhere in that neighborhood because that's where they hung out.

I remember one night, a B.A. came to Pak's on 5th Avenue to buy some beer. When he came out, a dude that didn't even hang at my house was with us at the store and started "plexing" (starting trouble) with the B.A. dude. He knocked him out cold. The B.A. dude's friends helped him back in the car and we left from the store and went back to our G-rage. We saw a car come down 11th Street and when it came closer to 4th, our street, the lights went off. That's when we realized that it was the same car that the B.A. from Pak's was in. By this time the dude was hanging out the window with a shotgun, just busting like a madman. That's how my childhood was—you had to be in survival mode constantly, even just walking to and from school.

By this time my cousin Daniel was in prison. He was hanging with some other dudes while an 85 year old woman was murdered. He was there, though he didn't do anything, but he wouldn't snitch on the others. He got a 20 year sentence and is still locked up to this day. They tried him as an adult when he turned 16 in 1998. As I think back to that, I can truly say thank God He kept me.

CHAPTER 6

GRANDMA GOES ON TO MEET THE LORD

In 1995, my grandma went on to be with the Lord. Honestly, something clicked inside me when she died. It's like I stopped caring about anything and everything. My sister's father also died around the same time. We moved over to Orange Street behind old K-mart where H.E.B is now and our house was known as the weed house. It was me, my mom, sister, brother and his daughter, his girlfriend and her daughter all living in one house. We didn't stay there long. Soon, my mom, my sister, and I moved to the Briarwoods Apartments, but my cousin and I had a spot we hustled out of on the south side of Texas City

THE DAY I ALMOST KILLED SOMEONE

I remember one day I went to my "potna" Kevin Hampton's house trying to "re-up" (buying more drugs to sell). This dude named Clifford Jones was standing outside my potna's house "short-stopping." (Trying to sell someone drugs before they get to their regular place of purchase)

I said, "Hey, where Kevin at?" He said, "He not here, wha's up?"

I said, "Ain't nothing up. I'm looking for Kevin." Somehow we started arguing and the dude spit in my face! Something clicked in me that I had never felt before. All I know was I wanted to kill him. I ran down the sidewalk to my brother's house and told him to give me his gun. He asked me about three times what happened but I was so mad and enraged by this time that I was cursing at my brother, telling him to give me his gun. He gave me the gun and I walked out of his house. The guy Clifford, that spit on me was sitting on the porch about three houses down. When I saw him I took off running toward him and raised the gun up to start shooting. Only problem is the gun was on safety. While I'm trying to get the safety off, he started running toward me and then ran between two houses. The gun fired while I continued to run frantically and kept on firing. I ran back around the house to cut him off. When I got to the back of the house, he slipped in the mud and was lying on the ground. So I ran up to him, put the gun to his head and squeezed the trigger. To my great surprise there was no loud bang—just "click, click, click, click."

In my mindless rage, I had completely unloaded the clip in the gun with the wild shooting. We just looked at each other and I took off running because I knew the cops were on their way. My "potna" Spike was there and saw me running. He picked me up and took me to my spot on the south side of Texas City. I grabbed some clothes and he dropped me off in Houston's 5th ward, at my dad's Colombian girlfriend, Cynthia's house. I lived there for a while until things cooled off in Texas City.

CHAPTER 7
PCP ENTERS MY LIFE

After things in Texas City cooled down, I moved back to my mom's on 5th Avenue N. I was 16 years old and already a loose cannon. I hustled out of my mom's house, sold weed, went to clubs, drank, and smoked PCP. When a person does PCP, it causes an inner anger to pop out. I was cursing my mom out and I think she was scared of me.

The year I started smoking PCP ("FRY", "Sherm", or "Wet") was crazy. It's late 1996 and early 1997 and I have two women pregnant at the same time. My first child was born September 16, 1997. My son's mom was living with me, along with my mom and my sister. My other child was a daughter, born December 15, 1997. My daughter's mother was seeing another man at that time so she told him that it was his daughter. For the first five to six years of my little girl's life, I didn't see her at all.

1997 was also the year I started my criminal record. I went to jail for the first time December 2, 1997 for criminal mischief. I smoked so much "Wet" one night I must have O. D.'d because I blacked out in the bathroom and when I came to, I was in the hospital.

After that, I went to jail March 12, 1998 for an assault causing bodily injury. I was at my "potna" Jim Bean's house. We called it the 5th Street Wet Set, where they sold the "Wet". This crackhead named Freddy Murdock stole my stash and somebody saw him do it. When I caught up with him I busted his head with a chain that had a lock on the end of it.

MY BUSINESS PARTNER—SHERMAN MARTINEZ

Around the same time I stopped selling crack and started selling weed again. I hooked up with a Mexican dude named Sherman Martinez who lived right down the street on 12th Street. We used to hustle pills, weed, and syrup. We got a connection with this white dude named Simon who had begun fronting us whatever we bought. I would buy 2 ½ pounds and Sherman would buy the same, equaling five pounds then Simon would credit us five pounds. One day I called Sherman and told him I was ready to "rescore", meaning I had sold all mine, so let's get some more. Sherman told me Simon said he couldn't front us anymore, at least not right now. This didn't sound right to me, so I called Simon on my own, because Simon and I were cool. I said, "What's good bro? I'm trying to spend this money with you. Do you got anything?" He said, "Hey I just dropped it off at Sherman's. He told me you were doing your own thing." I said, "Oh yeah?"and hung up the phone and went straight over to Sherman's house. I was used to being over there all day so I didn't think anything of just walking right in without knocking. I walked in and saw his mom on the couch in the living room. When I asked where Sherman was, she pointed to his room. When I went in there were about six Mexican dudes in his room smoking and chilling. I told Sherman to come holla at me outside, but he stood up and said, "I'm not going nowhere", so I acted like I was going to walk off and turned around and punched him hard as I could in his mouth and I just kept punching him. A couple of the Mexican dudes started to punch me, then

Sherman's stepdad, Will, came in the room, grabbed me and put my hands behind my back while the others punched me and threw me out the back door. I ran to my house down the street as fast as I could, grabbed my gun, and ran back. First I shot up Will's car, then I started shooting in the window in Sherman's room. I don't remember exactly what I did after that, but I was never caught for it. About six months later, Sherman and I sat down and talked it out and became best friends again.

Doc Amey

CHAPTER 8

HOW I LOST MY TEETH

I had taken five or six Xanax pills at one time. My cousin Jeremiah was in his car about to go somewhere, and I asked him if I could go with him. He said no so I jumped on the hood of his car. He hit the gas a little bit and started turning his steering wheel really fast and threw me off the car. I hit the concrete pavement face first and all my upper front teeth were knocked out. I had teeth stuck in my upper lip for months because I didn't go to the hospital and had no insurance. I remember running to my house to get a starter gun I had there. This was my cousin so I didn't want to shoot him for real. I just wanted to scare him and I knew he'd been shot before and that would scare him. People would know I would bust that hammer if I needed to so I hid behind my Aunt Kim's house until Jeremiah got in his car. I ran up to the car, stuck the gun in the window and started shooting. The look on his face was that of pure fright or terror, like he had met his maker. I unloaded the gun and took off running back to my house. I know you're wondering about Jeremiah, and if he was hurt. No, the bullets were fake. But I just wanted to scare him anyway. I didn't hang around to find out how furious he was at me.

Doc Amey

CHAPTER 9

LIVING IN SOUTH PARK APARTMENTS

It was around 1998 and 1999 and I was now living with my mom, my brother, and my sister. This period held some of the craziest times of my life. We are hustling "out the crib" like always, but now we had money for real or so we thought. When you're making money that's when it's easy to get greedy. The crazy thing is that out of all the people for me to bump heads with it was my own brother. We fought like total strangers. It seemed like he was buddies with everybody else but me. He treated me like he didn't know me. I was cool with that because I was getting money just like them.

My "potna" Busy used to sell "Wet" and this dude wanted Busy to dip a Swisher cigar in "Wet" rolled with weed in it. As Busy was dipping the cigar it fell into the bottle of "Wet" and absorbed much more than it should have. Busy says "Man we not gonna sell this one!" He wrapped it up in foil and I put it in the freezer. This happened early in the day and I was already wasted. At ten o'clock that night, I asked my Uncle Craig to sell some cigars rolled with weed for me.
At first he tells me no. I must have begged him for over 30 minutes, so he finally said yes. I was going to my oldest daughter's mother's house that night. Right as I was getting in my car to leave, Busy pulls up and says,

"Wha's up—you gone smoke that Swisher dipped in

"Wet" with me?" I was already intoxicated to the max. I had totally forgotten about the "Fry stick" in the freezer. I went and got it and fired it up. It tasted like I had swallowed some anti-freeze and felt like my lungs literally froze up. We were sitting there smoking and talking. We got about halfway through and I was done. I jumped in my car and smashed off. I don't know how I made it all the way to Gulf Breeze Apts. on Main in LaMarque, Texas, but I did. I got to my daughter's mother's and I am wired up on this "Wet", so I took a couple of Soma pills and some Xanax bars to come down. I took a shower. As I'm relaxing, my pager goes off. It's my mom's number with 911 after it, meaning emergency.

I called my mom and she tells me my uncle went to jail and all he kept saying was call Doc. I told my daughter's mom that my uncle is in jail and I have to get him out. She told me no and she insisted on driving because I was too messed up. I convinced her that I was okay, so I jumped in my car and headed to Texas City going down Main. Once you cross Hwy 146 and Main St., then you are by the refineries, so I must have been doing pretty good. If I would have fallen asleep where the road kind of curves, I would have run straight into the train back there. At the end of the road you either go right to Galveston or left to Texas City. I did neither. I fell asleep behind the wheel, went straight, hit the curb, and went over a 24 ft gas line, down into a 20 ft ditch at the bottom. When I hit the curb it woke me up and when I looked around everything was pitch black. My car nosedived down into the ditch and my dashboard was up to my neck. My back seat was literally in my front seat. They said if I had been ten pounds heavier I would have been crushed in the car. I was able to walk away with no scratches!

Water was up to my stomach in the car. I looked around. It was dark and I had no clue where I was. I finally managed to get out of my car and my right tire was still rolling down the bank of the ditch, my battery and my other tire was in the water as well. The front end of the car was literally smashed in from the impact. It took me a little while to get out of the ditch because I was soaking wet and so intoxicated, but I walked to the street and a truck driver picked me up. He took me about 50 ft. When he saw the police, he told me I had to get out of his truck. As soon as I got out, the police drew down on me, hogtied me, and put me in the back of the police car. When we got to the police station, I asked the jailer if they had Craig Amey, my uncle. I asked them to put me in his cell. As soon as I got in there, he started cursing and talking about how I begged him to keep the weed and sell it and if I had just left him alone neither of us would be in this predicament. Mind you, I was so intoxicated out of this world from uppers and downers, so all I heard was "blah, blah, blah, blah". I only know about this because we talked about it when I sobered up.

So that night, though I paid for us to get out, they made Uncle Craig stay because he had some unpaid tickets. I called a cab and went and rented a room at the Econo Lodge on Texas Avenue. I bought a gallon of milk and soaked in hot water trying to come down. I called my "potna" Busy and told him where I was and the room number and asked him to bring me some weed.

When I spoke with Busy on the phone, he sounded super excited to talk to me. I couldn't figure out why until later when he got to my room with "Big Homie" D-Ray. They saw the wrecker pulling my car out of the ditch when they were headed back from club. From the looks of the car, they just knew I was either in the hospital or worse--dead. So we sat in the room and got high on the same drugs I was attempting to come down from earlier that morning. That was our life.

I got them to take me by the wrecker later because I had some "stuff" in my trunk that I really needed to get. Yes, more drugs. I told the wrecker man which car is mine and that I would like to get something out of the car. The first words out of his mouth were, "How's the driver of this car?" I said, "You lookin' at him", and I think he thought I was joking since I was smiling at him. So he asked me again, "No really, how's the driver?" I said, "You looking at him!" He said, "Son, my father has been in the wrecking business for 50 plus years and over 30 years for me and we have never seen anybody walk away from a wreck of this magnitude." He said, "Son, did you thank God when you woke up this morning?" I said, "Yes I did, and it was not a lie."

I thought back to my cousin Kenny, "Big Kenny". I was about 14, already trying to buy drugs for myself. At 8am that morning I wanted some "syrup" and not the kind you put on pancakes. I called and called until Big Kenny finally made it to his dope spot. I will never forget what he said, "Man, you rushin' me to sell you this drank (codeine syrup). Did you thank God when you woke up this morning?" It shocked me because I'd never woke up and thanked God for waking me. He said, "From now on when you wake up, the first thing you need to say is, 'Lord, I thank you for waking me up, please give me the strength to go on through this day'." With Big Kenny being someone I really looked up to, that really stuck to me. At 35 years of age now that's still first thing I say every time I wake up. Even drug dealers and users can call on God and trust Him to protect and watch over them. They may not know it, but God wants to deliver them out of their bondage! He's just waiting for a small crack in the door. When they pray this, it brings Almighty God into the action! I turned and told the wrecker, "I learned to thank God every morning from my cousin, Big Kenny." He then told me there is nothing in the car. The police already searched it so if you're trying to get anything out of the car, it's gone. He said that the way my car looked and how smashed the front end was, it looked like I could have been 30-40 feet in the air when the wreck occurred. I told him that I thought I was flying last night. My buddies and I were laughing and the man said," I don't think you realize or understand how serious this situation is. If you would have hit that big orange gas line in the ditch, you would have blown up things from here all the way to Baytown. That gas line runs underground."

I let that sink in and was like "Wow!" God was even then protecting me even though the enemy was trying to kill me and he almost succeeded. I realize now that the plans God had, and still has, for my life are very important, far beyond what I can imagine. For many years I just thought I was lucky. That night God spared my life, but I just kept right on living for myself. Someone told me I wouldn't live to see 25 if I kept going way the way I was going. That stuck with me even though I didn't plan on changing.

CHAPTER 10

"LITTLE BABY STAY-GONE"

I was not getting along well with my brother. We are all out hustling out of one house in South Park and my brother and I fought like complete strangers. Things started happening—I was sipping codeine syrup "drank", smoking weed, popping pills (Xanax), and smoking "Wet" (PCP). My life was a wreck. There was a lot of gambling going on, shooting dice. One night we were gambling and I had sold all my drugs because I was using and abusing all the drugs I was selling. My cousin Knott used to call me "Little Baby Stay-Gone" because every time he saw me, no matter what time of day it was, I was gone off them drugs. I couldn't even walk or talk sometimes. I use to wake up at different people's houses with my pockets turned inside out because I'd been "jacked". I was slipping and that had become the norm for me, so I tried not to pack money on me. One night I had sold all my drugs and lost all my money, so I couldn't buy more. Rent was coming due and my brother and I were fighting, and I didn't know what to do anymore. I went to a local club at the time called Low-Key aka Killa Key because a few people had gotten killed right outside the club. I was already loaded, intoxicated to the max, and I was sitting in the club smoking and just chilling. I ran across a dude named Bonz that I knew just casually from seeing him around. He was a rapper and I was also rapping. I was with a group called "No Luv Click". Truly, that's exactly what I got from them, no love. So, me and the dude Bonz started "chopping it up" (talking) and I told him what was going on with me and my situation. He said, "Hey man, I got a three bedroom house on Oleander in LaMarque if you need somewhere to go." We left the club that night, went to my brother's spot, grabbed all my clothes, and went and stayed with Bonz for a while.

DEALING CRACK

I never really like to sell crack cocaine because of the hours of business, but that's what Bonz did. When I got to his house he gave me a handful of crack and told me I didn't owe him anything. So now I'm a crack dealer. I made enough money off the crack to go back to Houston to the crooked doctors who would sell prescriptions that I could take to the pharmacy and get filled for pills and codeine syrup. This time period was also my introduction to Ecstasy, a drug I'd never used before. Things started to happen and I started to see cops rolling by Bonz house all hours of day and night. I knew I had to get away from there.

Fortunately, my mother got a duplex on 2nd Avenue in the Chelsea and she let me come live with her. This was the end of '99 and going into 2000 and I'm still doing the same things I always did—hustling, getting high, and just doing my thing, making trouble. My cousin, Trey, pops up and tells me that he is getting syrup (codeine) and hydro marijuana, street named "Dro". It's the top of the line best stuff you can get, so that set my business on top of the food chain because other people that were selling syrup were "stepping on it" to stretch it.(stepping on it means to dilute it to make more)   It was a high commodity but I was getting mine straight from California. I wasn't cutting mine because my pops William taught me quality beats quantity any day. I'd rather have a little bit of the good than a whole lot of trash. That went on for quite a while then my mom ended up moving back to South Park, but across the street from my brother.

CHAPTER 11

BROTHERLY LOVE?

I was back on my feet again, so my brother was now my competition. We would always get into it because deep down inside, I wanted so much for him to treat me right and give me the same love he gave his home boys. He would do things like ordering pizza and asking everyone to put in on it. He told me I couldn't have any if I didn't put in some money. He would take my money and I know nobody else put anything in. Slowly but surely, a hatred for him developed, one that I didn't think was possible because all I ever wanted was for my big brother to show me love like he did everybody else. I started hanging with older dudes, seeking that big brother love. I never hung out with dudes that were my age. Number 1, they are trouble, number 2, I was trying to fill a void of acceptance from a big brother. The thing that hurt me the worst was I was the only one he did that way. He never argued or so much as had a fight with anyone else but me. I got to a point in my life that I didn't see him as my brother but just another dude from the street to me. And in the streets it was all about respect, which I didn't get from him.

We are living across the street from my brother and both of us had sweet houses. We would roll weed up in Swisher sweet cigars and sell them out of our houses which were known as sweet houses. We were doing okay for a while then the Law came and kicked in our door at my mom's house. I was outside next door, watching the whole thing. The policeman came up behind me and put his gun to my head, and ordered me to get on my knees.

He didn't know what I might have on me but he knows I am known for packing guns. Not fun! They ended up finding a pound of weed and since the apartment was in my mom's name, they brought her from work and asked if they could search the place. It was my cousin Dan's weed so his little brother took the case. I knew I wasn't going to take it. My cousin Dan and a couple more dudes I will not name because they are still in the game, had a spot in Huntsville, Texas. With their traveling back and forth from Texas City to Huntsville, they needed somebody they could trust to be there in case someone tried to steal their weed while they were gone.

Selling in Huntsville

I went to Huntsville for a while and it was totally different. Those boys were so behind the times it was crazy. They were still doing things the way we did them in '95. We were getting over on them. There were prison guards coming to buy from us when we went to the clubs and we were like celebrities in the town. Everybody was letting us have our way, but then the other local dudes started hating on us because we were taking their money. The police started messing with us because of this. I was ready to leave and go back to Texas City. I wasn't trying to get myself in jail in Huntsville!

CHAPTER 12

BACK HOME AGAIN

I moved back to Texas City and my mom was living on 7th Avenue in the Chelsea again. My brother was living right next door! It was a disaster waiting to happen for me. I started going to the doctors in Houston again getting the codeine syrup and the pills for a cheap price and selling them for a very high price. It wasn't long till I found myself in jail. I caught a "possession for marijuana" charge June 6, 2000 and I also had pills on me when I was arrested. This added a "possession of dangerous drugs" (Xanax) charge the same day.

MORE BROTHERLY LOVE?

The tension between me and my brother was so thick, something happened between us and we were getting into it bad. My buddy Chris came to pick me up. Chris parked in front of my brother's house and when I got into the car, my brother smashed a 6 foot 4x4 thick wooden log through Chris's front driver and passenger window. If we wouldn't have noticed in time, he would have smashed Chris's head. He cranked up the car and took off with a big wooden log hanging out his window. We went to Chris's house and ,I will never forget, he had a 410 one-shot shotgun. You had to reload it after every shot. I got the gun and about ten bullets, put them in my pocket. I called and got me some "Wet" to smoke because I was planning to kill my brother. I smoked half of it then pulled up to my brother's house and peeked through the side window to see who all was in the house. When I looked through I saw my mom in there, and that was the only thing that kept me from shooting into that house at that moment. I waited well over 2 hours just sitting at the side of the house. I almost gave myself away because I fired that "wet" square back up and my mom smelled it. She said, "I smell 'wet'". So my brother got up and looked out his front door to see if anybody was on his porch smoking. I was watching him the whole time and started to shoot him right then, but my mom was still in the house.

About 30 minutes later I heard my mom say she was going to check on her clothes. My brother had a washer and dryer on his back porch. My adrenaline was pumping because I was about to shoot right then as she was walking to the back porch with her back toward me. My brother and his girlfriend (now his wife) were sitting right in front of the tv. He was sitting between her legs when I opened the screen door with one hand and held the gun in the other. My brother kicked his door closed with his foot. It hit the gun and turned it to the left as I was pulling the trigger. I shot the back of his big screen tv out and by this time his girlfriend was yelling, my mama was yelling, and I know he was trying to go to his room to get his gun. On the side of the house were two more windows in the living room. I shot them out and ran to the back yard. His bedroom had a big glass sliding window. The lighting in the room was perfect so that I could see a perfect silhouette of his body and I just started shooting through the window. I heard him say, "I'm hit! I'm hit!" I was using <u>bird shot(?)</u>, so he wasn't killed. I took off running through the trails back to my buddy Chris's house. We went to Galveston and stayed at his aunt's house in the Back Bay Apts till things cooled off.

Doc Amey

CHAPTER 13

BIG SHIRLEY AND SHOOTING DICE--2001

One night several guys were next door at my brother's spot. We were upstairs shooting dice and of course I was highly intoxicated. There was a dude there named "Big Shirley" who was selling drugs for my brother. I had hit my point, meaning the number I was trying to get before a 7 showed up. When I hit my point, "Big Shirley" noticed and quickly tried to cover the dice and to say he caught them. After a shooter shoots the dice, whoever has him "faded" (betting against you) can cover the dice before they stop rolling and that roll wouldn't count. If you let the dice stop and a person sees their points, then it's "point seen and money gone." I said, "Point seen and money gone!" I started to grab my money, but he had hurried to snatch the money before I did. He was gambling with my brother's money, that's why he was trying so hard not to lose.

We started yelling and cursing at each other and Big Shirley was much bigger than I was. He told me either I shoot it over or just consider it money lost. I punched him and we started tussling. We were right next to the stairs when he punched me and pushed me down the stairs. The same rage rose up in me as the day Clifford Jones spit in my face. I looked up from the bottom of the stairs and told Big Shirley, "I'm going to kill you!" That was along with a few more choice words. I left, went next door to my mom's and found a nice sized steak knife. I didn't want to use my gun—this was personal. I wanted to feel his blood on my hands. So I waited. I found myself some "wet" and smoked it and let everyone leave, then I went around to my brother's back door to use the washer and dryer to stand on and climb up the balcony to get upstairs. I peeked through the sheet hanging over the door and went through. The same way my brother was sitting between his girlfriend's legs, so were Big Shirley and his girlfriend, watching tv. I came through the curtain with the knife in my hand. You know how they say hesitation can get you killed, this is what happened with Big Shirley. He was paralyzed when he saw me and couldn't move. I went over to him and started stabbing him in the chest near his heart and lungs. Then I left before the Law could get there. I don't remember where I went, but those questioned told the police they didn't know who it was and my brother told them the same thing. This is the way of the streets. You don't snitch on anyone to the police. I was guilty, but I got off once again without any attempted murder charges. And God once again kept me from killing someone and ruining my life.

ESCAPED CHARGES FOR THIRD ASSAULT

Later that year my brother and I were at it, still crossways with each other. I had been in Houston all day, "busting scripts" (getting prescriptions) and I was upstairs at my mom's house. Man, I remember it like it was yesterday. I had just picked up some food from Wendy's. I had it all laid out with ketchup on my fries and everything ready to be devoured. Somebody told my brother that I was upstairs, and ,before I knew it, I could hear him running up the stairs. I thought to myself, "Here we go again." He busted in the door hollering and cursing. I stood up and we started arguing. He looked at the table where my food was and did a clean swipe as he knocked everything off the table. I felt that feeling of uncontrollable rage rise up in me. I grabbed a long knife out of the dish rack next to the sink, and when I did, my brother got a chair from the table with the legs out toward me. I was standing with my back to the sink and he had his back to the wall. It was like a stand-off for about 30 seconds, then he made his move to try to pin me against the sink with the chair. I ducked the chair and he extended his arms so I came up between him and the chair. I grabbed him with my right arm to pull him to me and I stabbed him with my left hand since I am left-handed. When I pulled the knife out all I had was the handle in my hand. He hit the wall and put a big hole in it and I ran down the stairs. Again I can't remember where I went and again no charges were filed against me. Once again the grace of God was on my life and kept me from killing my brother. I didn't understand it because with three attempted murders, they could have buried me under the jail if they'd had formal charges against me. However, I still didn't learn my lesson. I was still doing my hustling, getting drugs, and the works.

CHAPTER 14

THE FIRES OF RAGE

Now it's around late 2000 or early 2001 and my oldest daughter's mom and I had hooked up again. She moved downstairs from my mom, next door to my brother's spot. One night I left my house on 7th to go to my "potna" Bo's house. He lived on the south side and I went to sell them some "drank". While I'm there I was sitting on the couch and they were telling everyone to get up, that there's some "drank" missing out of the freezer. Everybody got up and there just so happened to be a small baby food jar with syrup in it right next to where I was sitting. They started saying I tried to steal their syrup. We were arguing and out of nowhere someone punched me and about six people were there jumping on me. I started running for the door and I was able to get out.

I heard two gunshots and suddenly that feeling of rage came over me again. I ran to the corner grocery and bought two bottles of Mexican soda and filled the bottles with gasoline. I tore my undershirt up and stuffed them in the bottles for wicks and made some Molotov cocktails. I ran back over there and when I knocked on the door nobody answered. I kicked the door open, lit one and threw it in the house. It seemed like the whole house flamed up instantly, so I just threw the other one in there too and hit the ground running as fast as I could back home. I jumped in the tub, but the whole time my daughter and her mom were in the bedroom asleep. They never knew I left the house. When the fire marshal came an hour later, my girlfriend swore I'd never left the house.

There is a pattern here of my disobedience and the grace of God somehow shielding me from my own self-destruction. Why couldn't I wake up?

WHEN I GOT SHOT—2001

This dude named Jim lived right across the street from me and he sold "wet". One day my "potna" Lewis (RIP) and I broke into his house. I climbed through the back window and unlocked the side door for my homeboy, Lewis. We found the "wet" and the weed in the kitchen and while leaving out the side door, someone was coming up the trail and saw us exiting the house. At that time I was on the "wet" so bad I was doing things like stealing and making shady drug deals just to support my habit. About three hours later, while I was smoking some of the "wet" we just jacked, I hear a bang on my door. I looked out the blinds and there were Jim and his wife. I told my girlfriend (my daughter's mom) to answer the door to see what he wanted. He told her he was looking for me and Lewis and he needed to talk to us. About an hour later, we went outside because Jim was just sitting outside on his car watching my house. Immediately after we went out he came to the edge of the street talking loud and cursing at us and he ran up on Lewis and started fighting. Jim was swinging but backing up towards his house the whole time. He was luring Lewis as close toward his car as he could so he could grab his shotgun. He got the shotgun from the side of the car and pointed it at us. My buddy was in the middle of the street and I was at the edge of my yard. Jim was standing in his driveway at his house, and I just remember Jim's wife telling him that we weren't worth it.

Lewis was yelling, "Go ahead and shoot, I'm not scared to die!" I heard like five loud bangs and after the third one, I knew my buddy was hit. He was running toward me but he could hardly stand up, so I grabbed him and about the fifth bang, I was hit also. It felt like red hot pellets all down the side of my body, in my hand, hip, leg, and knee.

By the time we got Lewis on the front porch of my house, it looked like he took one solid shot to his front torso. You could literally see pellet holes everywhere from the top of his head and all down his legs. They rushed him to the hospital and he recovered, only to be murdered, gunned down, seven years later while coming out of a sports bar.

Doc Amey

SECTION 2

GRACE RAN OUT

CHAPTER 15

GRACE RAN OUT

On the list of my charges, on the following page, you can see all the times I went to jail for weed, pills, and running from the cops. Those were only the things I got caught for! I got away with three times more than that! On Sept 8, 2001, I caught a possession for cocaine and on Feb 2, 2002 (2-2-02) I caught a possession of a controlled substance (hydrocodone\ Vicodin). I felt that my grace had run out because I wasn't doing anything bad that night. I came out of my house downstairs and went to my mom's house upstairs. All of a sudden I heard my mom's back door burst wide open and all I heard was a policeman saying, "Get down". I ran into my sister's room and threw my pills behind the door as I went and walked out of the room with my hands up. They put me in handcuffs and went back and found the pills. They had me in the living room while they searched the whole house. They came out of my mom's room with all kinds of drugs. Those were my first two felony convictions.

COUNTY of GALVESTON
District Clerk
JOHN D. KINARD

Certificate of Criminal Record Search
Record Found

Date of Search: MARCH 12, 2015
Name Searched: EDWARD DEMONT AMEY
AKA: EDWARD DEMOND AMEY
AKA: DOC AMEY

Date of Birth: FEBRUARY 9, 1980

Last 4 Digits of Social Security Number: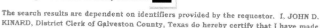

The search results are dependent on identifiers provided by the requestor. I, JOHN D. KINARD, District Clerk of Galveston County, Texas do hereby certify that I have made a diligent search of the records of this office for a period from January 1, 1984 to MARCH 11, 2015, or the name and identifiers provided above.

A CRIMINAL RECORD WAS FOUND INVOLVING THE ABOVE NAMED PERSON AS DEFENDANT STYLED:

Cause Number: 01CR1691; The State of Texas VS EDWARD DEMOND AMEY; Filed in the 122ND District Court of Galveston County, Texas.

Cause Number: 01CR1692; The State of Texas VS EDWARD DEMOND AMEY; Filed in the 122ND District Court of Galveston County, Texas.

Cause Number: 02CR0348; The State of Texas VS EDWARD DEMOND AMEY; Filed in the 122ND District Court of Galveston County, Texas.

Cause Number: 02CR1658; The State of Texas VS EDWARD DEMOND AMEY; Filed in the 122ND District Court of Galveston County, Texas.

Cause Number: 04CR0979; The State of Texas VS EDWARD DEMOND AMEY; Filed in the 10TH District Court of Galveston County, Texas.

Cause Number: 06CR3706; The State of Texas VS EDWARD DEMOND AMEY; Filed in the 122ND District Court of Galveston County, Texas.

www.co.galveston.tx.us/district_clerk
600 59th Street, Suite 4001 • GALVESTON, TEXAS 77551

KEPT

P/G - NOLO - TDCJ/SJ

NO. 02CR0348

02 JUL -8 AM 11:04

THE STATE OF TEXAS

VS.

EDWARD DEMOND AMEY

IN THE DISTRICT COURT OF
GALVESTON COUNTY, TEXAS
122ND JUDICIAL DISTRICT

JUDGMENT ON PLEA OF GUILTY OR NOLO CONTENDERE BEFORE COURT
WAIVER OF JURY TRIAL

Judge Presiding: Frank Carmona
Date of Plea: June 17, 2002
Date of Judgment: July 8, 2002
Attorney for State: Larry Drosnes   Attorney for Defendant: David McCormack

Offense Convicted Of: Possession of a controlled substance, to-wit: Hydrocodone as reduced from Possession of a controlled substance, to-wit: Hydrocodone with intent to Deliver [481.115 Health and Safety Code]

Degree: Second   Date Offense Committed: February 22, 2002

Charging Instrument: INDICTMENT   Plea: GUILTY

Terms of Plea Bargain (In Detail): Three (3) years Institutional Division of the Texas Department of Criminal Justice

Plea to Enhancement Paragraph(s): n/a

Findings on Enhancement: n/a

Findings on Use of Deadly Weapon: n/a

Date Sentence Imposed: July 8, 2002   Court Costs: $ 228⁰⁰

Punishment and
Place of Confinement: Three (3) years Institutional Division of the Texas Department of Criminal Justice

Date to Commence: July 8, 2002

State Jail Sentence to Begin: ( ) on _____
( ) Upon admission of Defendant into the facility.

Attorney Fees: $ _____   Fine: $ _____

Victim Restitution: $ _____   Crime Stoppers: $ 25.00

County Jail Time Credit: 16 days

State Jail Time Credit: _____

TOTAL AMOUNT OF RESTITUTION/
REPARATION: SEE ATTACHMENT "A"
INCORPORATED HEREIN BY
REFERENCE FOR ALL PURPOSES

Concurrent Unless Otherwise Specified. _____

(*) AS STATED OR SHOWN ON FRONT PAGE AND INCORPORATED HEREIN.

On (*) the above entitled and numbered cause was called for trial and the State appeared by her Assistant Criminal District Attorney, (*), and the

Doc Amey

P/G - NOLO - TDCJ/SJ

NO. 01CR1692

02 JUL -8 AM 11:03

THE STATE OF TEXAS

VS.

EDWARD DEMOND AMEY

IN THE DISTRICT COURT OF
GALVESTON COUNTY, TEXAS
122ND JUDICIAL DISTRICT

JUDGMENT ON PLEA OF GUILTY OR NOLO CONTENDERE BEFORE COURT
WAIVER OF JURY TRIAL

Judge Presiding: Frank Carmona
Date of Plea: June 17, 2002
Date of Judgment: July 8, 2002

Attorney for State: Larry Drosnes   Attorney for Defendant: David McCormack

Offense Convicted Of: Possession of a controlled substance, to-wit: Cocaine [481.115 Health and Safety Code]

Degree: Second   Date Offense Committed: September 8, 2001

Charging Instrument: INDICTMENT   Plea: GUILTY

Terms of Plea Bargain (In Detail): Three (3) years Institutional Division of the Texas Department of Criminal Justice

Plea to Enhancement Paragraph(s): n/a

Findings on Enhancement: n/a

Findings on Use of Deadly Weapon: n/a

Date Sentence Imposed: July 8, 2002   Court Costs: $ 216.00

Punishment and Place of Confinement: Three (3) years Institutional Division of the Texas Department of Criminal Justice

Date to Commence: July 8, 2002

State Jail Sentence to Begin: ( ) on _____
( ) Upon admission of Defendant into the facility.

Attorney Fees: $ _____   Fine: $ _____

Victim Restitution: $ _____   Crime Stoppers: $ 25.00

County Jail Time Credit: 26 days

State Jail Time Credit: _____

TOTAL AMOUNT OF RESTITUTION/REPARATION: SEE ATTACHMENT "A" INCORPORATED HEREIN BY REFERENCE FOR ALL PURPOSES

Concurrent Unless Otherwise Specified. _____

(*) AS STATED OR SHOWN ON FRONT PAGE AND INCORPORATED HEREIN.

On (*) the above entitled and numbered cause was called for trial and the State appeared by her Assistant Criminal District Attorney, (*), and the Defendant herein, appeared in person by his attorney, (*), and all parties

KEPT

P/G - NOLO - TDCJ/SJ
[JUDG1] [REV. 12/99]

NO. 02CR1658

THE STATE OF TEXAS   IN THE DISTRICT COURT OF

VS.   GALVESTON COUNTY, TEXAS

EDWARD DEMOND AMEY   122ND JUDICIAL DISTRICT

**JUDGMENT ON PLEA OF GUILTY OR NOLO CONTENDERE BEFORE COURT
WAIVER OF JURY TRIAL**

Judge Presiding: Frank Carmona   Date of Judgment: September 10, 2002
Attorney for State: Larry Drosnes   Attorney for Defendant: David Subler

Offense Convicted Of: Possession of a controlled substance, to-wit: Phencyclidine
[481.115 Health and Safety Code]

Degree: State Jail   Date Offense Committed: June 15, 2001

Charging Instrument: INDICTMENT   Plea: GUILTY

Terms of Plea Bargain (In Detail): One (1) year State Jail Division of the Texas Department of Criminal Justice

Plea to Enhancement Paragraph(s): n/a

Findings on Enhancement: n/a

Findings on Use of Deadly Weapon: n/a

Date Sentence Imposed: September 10, 2002   Court Costs: $ 208.00

Punishment and   One (1) year State Jail
Place of Confinement: Division of the Texas Department of Criminal Justice

Date to Commence: September 10, 2002

State Jail Sentence to Begin: (X) on September 10, 2002
                              ( ) Upon admission of Defendant into the facility.

Attorney Fees: $ Indigent   Fine: $ _____

Victim Restitution: $ _____   Crime Stoppers: $ 25.00

County Jail Time Credit: _____
State Jail Time Credit: since 6-21-02

TOTAL AMOUNT OF RESTITUTION/
REPARATION: SEE ATTACHMENT "A"
INCORPORATED HEREIN BY
REFERENCE FOR ALL PURPOSES

Concurrent Unless Otherwise Specified. _____

(*) AS STATED OR SHOWN ON FRONT PAGE AND INCORPORATED HEREIN.

On (*) the above entitled and numbered cause was called for trial and the

Doc Amey

P-G NOLO COURT PUNISH - CJ 12.44 P.C. (DRUGS) [DS2-C]

CAUSE NO. 04CR0979 (_____) TRN #901-230-8976-A001

THE STATE OF TEXAS	§	IN THE 10TH JUDICIAL
V.	§	DISTRICT COURT OF
EDWARD DEMOND AMEY,	§	GALVESTON COUNTY, TEXAS
DEFENDANT		
SID: TX _____		

JUDGMENT OF CONVICTION BY COURT; SENTENCE TO GALVESTON COUNTY JAIL

DATE OF JUDGMENT: June 14, 2004
JUDGE PRESIDING: David E. Garner
ATTORNEY FOR THE STATE: Charles Dunkel, Jr.
ATTORNEY FOR THE DEFENDANT: Enid Williams
OFFENSE: Possession of a Controlled Substance, to-wit: MDMA
STATUTE FOR OFFENSE: Article _____, Section 481.116, Health and Safety Code
DEGREE OF OFFENSE: State Jail Felony-Sec. 12.44 (a), PC
APPLICABLE PUNISHMENT RANGE
  (including enhancements, if any): State Jail 180 days-2 yrs/Max $10,000 Fine
DATE OF OFFENSE: April 17, 2004
CHARGING INSTRUMENT: Indictment
PLEA TO OFFENSE: Guilty
PLEA TO ENHANCEMENT
  PARAGRAPH(S): Not Applicable
VERDICT FOR OFFENSE: Guilty
FINDING ON ENHANCEMENT: Not Applicable
AFFIRMATIVE FINDING ON
  DEADLY WEAPON: Not Applicable
OTHER AFFIRMATIVE
  SPECIAL FINDINGS: Not Applicable
  (see full text below)
DATE SENTENCE IMPOSED: June 14, 2004
PUNISHMENT AND PLACE
OF CONFINEMENT: One year(x) Galveston County Jail

COUNTY JAIL TIME CREDITED
  TO SENTENCE: Since 04/17/2004
COURT COSTS: $ 258.00   ATTORNEY FEES: $ 330.60
AMOUNT OF FINE: $ _____   CRIME STOPPERS: $ 25.00
EXTRADITION COSTS: $ _____
TOTAL AMOUNT OF
  RESTITUTION: $ _____

KEPT

P-NG JURY FOUND GUILTY COURT PUNISH TDCJ-SJ-CJ [DS3]

CAUSE NO. 06CR3706 (_____) TRN #901-273-3219 A001

2008 FEB 21 PM 4:37

THE STATE OF TEXAS	§	IN THE 122ND JUDICIAL
V.	§	DISTRICT COURT OF
EDWARD DEMOND AMEY,	§	GALVESTON COUNTY, TEXAS
DEFENDANT		
SID: TX 05934700		

JUDGMENT OF CONVICTION BY JURY; SENTENCE BY COURT TO INSTITUTIONAL DIVISION, TDCJ

DATE OF JUDGMENT:	February 21, 2008
JUDGE PRESIDING:	Frank Carmona
ATTORNEY FOR THE STATE:	James Haugh
ATTORNEY FOR THE DEFENDANT:	Stephen Taylor
OFFENSE:	**Unlawful Possession of a Firearm by a Felon with enhancement**
STATUTE FOR OFFENSE:	Article _____, Section 46.04, Penal Code
DEGREE OF OFFENSE:	Second Degree Felony as Enhanced
APPLICABLE PUNISHMENT RANGE	
(including enhancements, if any):	Second Degree 2-20 yrs in prison/max $10,000 Fine
DATE OF OFFENSE:	December 12, 2006
CHARGING INSTRUMENT:	Indictment
PLEA TO OFFENSE:	Not Guilty
PLEA TO ENHANCEMENT	
PARAGRAPH(S):	True to enhancement paragraph
VERDICT FOR OFFENSE:	Guilty
FINDING ON ENHANCEMENT:	True to enhancement paragraph
AFFIRMATIVE FINDING ON	
DEADLY WEAPON:	Not Applicable,
OTHER AFFIRMATIVE	
SPECIAL FINDINGS:	Not Applicable
(see full text below)	
DATE SENTENCE IMPOSED:	February 21, 2008
PUNISHMENT AND PLACE	
OF CONFINEMENT:	**Five (5) year(s) Institutional Division of the Texas Department of Criminal Justice, and a $ -0- fine**

COUNTY JAIL TIME CREDITED
TO SENTENCE: 07/30/07 - 07/31/07, 05/17/07 to 06/03/07, 12/13/06 to 01/17/07

COURT COSTS:	$ 301.00	ATTORNEY FEES:	$ 2790.00
AMOUNT OF FINE:	$ _____	CRIME STOPPERS:	$ 25.00
EXTRADITION COSTS:	$ _____		
TOTAL AMOUNT OF RESTITUTION:	$ _____		

53

Doc Amey

The County of Galveston
P.O. Box 17253
Galveston County Justice Center
Galveston, Texas 77552

Dwight D. Sullivan
County Clerk

March 11, 2015

I, Dwight D. Sullivan, County Clerk of Galveston County do hereby certify that I have made a diligent search of the records of this office for a period from **January 1, 1984** to on or about March 11, 2015 for **Edward Demont Amey DOB: 02/09/1980** and find the following filed on the above named person. However, I do not guarantee the correctness thereof.

Misdemeanor:

MD-0173835 Criminal Mischief $20<$500 filed 12/02/1997 received on 05/27/1998 Dismissal request of complaining witness

MD-0176127 Assault Causes Bodily Injury filed 03/12/1998 received on 05/27/1998 $199.25 court cost/$500 fine/365 days jail probated for 12 months probation/ guilty. defendant pled true on 06/15/2000 defendant received 30days jail 20 days credit plus court cost

MD-0197495 Possession Marijuana filed 06/06/2000 received on 06/07/2000 $275.25 court cost/ 20days jail/ 13 days credit/ NOLO

MD-0197497 Possession Dangerous Drug filed on 06/06/2000 received on 06/07/2000 Dismissal Defendant convicted in case #197495

MD-0208857 Possession Dangerous Drug filed on 09/24/2001 received on 09/12/2002 Dismissal Defendant convicted in another case

MD-0209827 Possession Marijuana filed on 10/29/2001 received on 09/12/2002 $200 court cost/180 days jail/ 103 days credit/guilty

MD-0209830 Evading Arrest Detention filed on 10/29/2001 received on 09/12/2002 Dismissal defendant convicted in another case

MD-0211810 Possession Dangerous Drug filed on 01/22/2002 received on 09/12/2002 Dismissal defendant convicted in another case

MD-0212728 Possession Dangerous Drug filed on 02/18/2002 received on 09/12/2002 $200.50 Court cost/ 200 jail time/103 credit

MD-0213061 Possession Dangerous Drug filed on 02/26/2002 received on 09/12/2002 Dismissal defendant convicted in another case

MD-0213607 Possession Dangerous Drug filed on 03/26/2002 received on 09/12/2002 $200 court cost/200 days jail/103 days credit

MD-0214141 Theft Property $50<$500 filed on 04/11/2002 received on 09/12/2002 $275 court cost/180 days jail/ 103 days credit

MD-0235947 Evading Arrest Detention filed on 07/29/2004 received on 07/30/2004 $276 court cost/100 days jail/107 days credit/ NOLO

MD-0260773 Possession Marijuana filed on 09/25/2006 received on 11/09/2006 Dismissal Interest of Justice

KEPT

MD-0263244 Possession Marijuana filed on 12/28/2006 received on 02/25/2008 Dismissal defendant pled to case 06cr3706

MD-0263271 Evading Arrest Detention filed on 12/28/2006 received on 02/25/2008 Dismissal Defendant pled to case 06cr3706

MD-0269376 Assault Causes Bodily Injury filed on 05/22/2007 received on 02/25/2008 Dismissal defendant pled to case 06cr3706

MD-0272612 Possession Marijuana filed on 08/03/2007 received on 02/25/2008 Dismissal defendant pled to case 06cr3706

There is no liability attached to the signing of this instrument.
Given under my hand and seal of office this **11th** day of **March**, 2015 at 12:57 o'clock p.m.

Dwight D. Sullivan, County Clerk
Galveston County, Texas

By: *Becky Hernandez*, Deputy Clerk
Becky Hernandez

GOING TO PRISON

On June 17, 2002, I was assigned and agreed to 3 years in TDC for both cases. July 8, 2002 the judgment came down and I turned myself in to start doing my time. This would be my first trip to prison but not my last. On the morning of October 8, 2002, 2 am, they called me out of my bunk and told me to pack my stuff that I was on the chain gang--that is "on my way to prison." I ended up at the back gate of the Holliday Unit with about 45 other men with cases ranging from drugs like mine all the way to double homicide.

This being my first time, I didn't know what to expect. I could only go by what I'd heard from people in the county jail who'd been there. You forget all that by the time you get there. When we walk in, there are four or five cages on the wall and they are already filled with men like caged animals. They lined us up 3 rows of 15. Right at the back door, as soon as you come in, they strip us all naked, make us lift both our feet one at a time, and lift our testicles, then the famous "bend over and cough". We were allowed to put our boxers back on, and one by one we walked up to this lady behind a fence in a chair who asked us medical questions. When we finished that, we had to go sit in a cage. From there, I could see the rest of the operation.

There were five officers standing behind a cage, three barber chairs, and three showers which were wide open for all to see you. On the other side of the showers were benches full of men with their whites on. This is the initial process. An officer from behind the gate would call an inmate's name to come look at the property the inmate had brought with him from the county jail. The officer would then tell the inmate what he could keep and what he couldn't keep. The inmate had the option of mailing his things home at his own expense, or having it thrown away. I already knew when I was in county jail that I was going to prison, so the day I "caught chain" (was sent to prison) I left everything that I knew I wouldn't be able to keep in prison. I had my kids' mother come get it. I say "kids" because I had another son born on September 11, 2002, while I was still in county jail.

When I went to the window, the officer gave me my blanket, clothes, pillowcase, etc. I looked down the line and saw one of the prison guards that used to buy drugs from me. I tried to get his attention but he acted like he didn't see me. After I got all my gear, I went and sat down in the barber chair and they cut my head completely bald just before they gave me a razor to shave all my facial hair. I had to go sit on the bench then and wait for my name to be called. My picture was taken and then I had to strip again so they could make note of all my tattoos and ask what each one meant.

The next thing on their agenda was for us to see a doctor in the medical division and answer all kinds of questions about our health. Then I reported to the residence to put away all my necessities given to me. Time now to eat.

With over 200 inmates in the chow hall it was a crazy scene. I got my food and sat down to eat. I saw dudes eating so fast it looked like they didn't even chew. I was so busy looking around trying to absorb it all, I didn't realize that after three minutes a guard came and knocked on our table and meal time was over! I found out really fast that means get up and throw your tray away. I barely ate that first day, but that was the first and last night I went to bed hungry. I'm a very fast learner, at least when it comes to food.

I had a very hard time going to sleep that first night being in such a place, and when I finally dozed off, an officer came in the dorm yelling at the top of his lungs, "Chow time! Chow time!" I found out that meant time to go eat, so I got up, washed my face, brushed my teeth, and went to breakfast.

There I was in prison—paying my dues to society for all the evil things I'd done, and all I could think about every day was getting out of that place. I stayed on the Holliday Unit for about six months, just long enough to get comfortable, then they shipped me to a private prison in Bridgeport, Texas between Dallas and Fort Worth. It was a very "chill" laid-back spot and I did very well there and ended up getting out late 2003 to early 2004.

FREE AGAIN BUT NOT FOR LONG--DICKINSON 2004

I moved in with my children's mother in Dickinson. I stayed out of trouble for a few months then I planned to go with some buddies to Kappa Beach party in Galveston. We got pulled over right as we got into Galveston. My buddy had an expired sticker on his car. On that day, April 17, 2004, I was arrested for possession of a controlled substance—MDMA, which was an Ecstasy pill that I had on me, and some Xanax pills. I was out of prison on parole so that's an automatic arrest. I sat in the county jail for about two months before I got bonded out. That should have been a big wake-up for me, but I kept on.

On July 29, 2004, the cops tried to stop me, but I had drugs on me, so I took off running, just long enough to throw the drugs down, and then was arrested for evading arrest that day. I was out the next day. I was still "doing ME" and violated my parole when I pled guilty for the April drug arrest.

Doc Amey

CHAPTER 16

BACK TO SQUARE ONE

I was walking through the back door of the Holliday Unit in Huntsville prison again on September 28, and the procedure was exactly the same as before—stripped, searched, hair cut off, caged, bent over and told to cough, etc. I stayed in Holiday for only about three months and this time they shipped me to the Segovia Unit in Edinburg, Texas, deep south aka "Little Mexico". Ninety percent of the prison population was Mexican or Spanish-speaking, so it was very rough for a black dude down there. Ninety-eight percent of the guards and officers were Hispanic. It was very hot and I was there in the summer—blazing hot! I learned one thing in prison—**you get in trouble, you go to jail. You don't go to jail to get in trouble** because if you do they can make your time very hard.

So, I was doing good, staying out of trouble. Then I stopped receiving mail from my kids' mother. I was writing but she wasn't responding. I was able to make a phone call because of good behavior, so I called my mom and asked her if she'd heard from her. The phone got deadly quiet and I said, "Hello!" My mom said, "She pregnant!" That hit me in the face like a ton of bricks. I felt betrayed, hurt and I totally lost faith in women at that point.

GOT MY GED

I stayed focused and got my GED on December 5, 2005. I got out of prison early the middle of 2006. I didn't have anywhere to go, and of all the people in the world, my brother let me come and stay with him for a little while until I was able to get on my feet. I caught a weed case (was arrested) September,25, 2006, but I got out of jail and continued to do my thing. I moved out to Sundance Apartments with my cousin Trina and I was hustling, and still getting high

THERE GOES CINDERELLA

Hurricane Katrina hit in 2005, which brought an influx of refugees. I ran into this in 2006 when I was released from prison and came home. A lot of the Louisiana refugees were living in Texas City and doing lots of robberies. My homeboys and I kept a gun with us and never walked around alone. We were always two or three together. One night it was my homeboy and me walking to Kroger to get some orange juice and plastic baggies. As we are walking I saw two cops by Taco Bell in the parking lot, and two on the other side by Big Lots with their lights on. I'm not doing anything wrong so I paid them no mind. When we got down the sidewalk by China Border, the two cop cars pull up to us, jump out of the car and tell us to freeze and put our hands up. I had a pistol and some drugs on me so I can't let them search me. I take off running and as I was running the pistol came out of my back pocket and hit my shoe

I lost the gun and my right shoe. I ran to my buddy's

house and he let me in. I was telling him what happened and his girlfriend comes in the living room, talking loudly and "tripping" saying how she was on probation and that I need to get out. I asked my other homeboy to go outside and check to see if the cops were around. He walked out and came back reporting that the coast is clear. Boy, was he wrong! I ran around the corner and took the stairs three at a time and was looking down as I ran. What I didn't know was they were up there waiting for me at another buddy's apartment. It was another person that led them there accidentally but the results were still the same. I was caught. The policeman, Sal Chapa, jokingly said, "There goes Cinderella!"

> *LITTLE DID I KNOW YEARS LATER GOD WOULD USE THIS ENCOUNTER TO SHOW THE WORLD HIS GLORY.*

THE COP AND THE CON BECOME BROTHERS IN CHRIST

The next morning Captain Joe Stanton was the officer who was doing the investigation on my gun case. As already stated, I've had lots of dealings with the TCPD. One thing I never did was to snitch on anybody and if I ever got caught by the police, I always confessed and told them the truth. I figure I'm already caught, what's the use in lying because if I'm caught lying, my one chance of getting them to go easy on me is out the window.

That morning while Captain Stanton was interrogating me, I told him everything from start to finish. When I told the judge to go ahead and take me to trial, thinking I would delay and get more time on the streets, the court used exactly what I told Capt. Stanton to convict me.

> *This story has a surprise ending though. When I started going to the Fellowship in 2012, I found out that Captain Joe Stanton and I were attending the same church! What could have been very awkward, God had already reconciled! We had not had much interaction until we both were at a men's fellowship cookout on Pastor Kevin's little ranch. We greeted each other and found ourselves with no ill feelings between us—the "Cop and the Con", now brothers in Christ! Only Jesus can accomplish that! We each gave our testimonies around the campfire that night and the guys were all amazed that we could have fellowship*

CHAPTER 17

NEW CHIEF IN TEXAS CLEANING UP THE STREETS

From around 1990-2007 in Texas City we had what we called "spots" and they were sometimes fully furnished apartments and sometimes we sold drugs from them. All the drug dealers in the town had spots that they would deal from to make money and have a convenient place for their customers to come to buy drugs. We hung out at these places. Some sold weed, others sold crack or "drank" syrup. They weren't nice places, just about $500 for the rental. It was easy to make $10-15 grand a month depending on the drug.

We had it pretty easy selling drugs in Texas City until 2006 when the new chief of police, came. By the end of the first year "spots" were no longer wise, in fact they were out of the question. Everyone had started working off their cell phones. By this time I had moved out to Fountain Lake Apts to get out of Texas City proper because this guy was not playing. He had ZERO tolerance for drug dealing in his town. Now the neighborhoods we used to dominate were like ghost towns and very quiet. At first I was not happy, because like everybody else, I saw it as stopping my flow of easy money. Now, I applaud him. I know there are lots of dudes that talk bad about him and slander his name, but not me. He's done an amazing job in Texas City with the TCPD.

CHARGES

The charge was unlawful possession of a firearm by a convicted felon. I bonded out a few days later and on December 28, 2006, I was arrested again for possession of marijuana and evading arrest. Running from the police didn't seem to be working for me. Now, I am out on bond, trying to stay clear of trouble, and I moved out to Fountain Lake with my Uncle Craig. I was working at Ryan's and hustling on the side. In May, 2007 I caught another possession of marijuana case and I was still out on bond for the pistol case.

I was out in Fountain Lakes complex hustling and a girl there named Amy would let me give her crack to "post up" (hang out at her apartment) and meet my customers there. Amy had used up all her crack and wanted more. I told her no that I had already paid her for the night and I wasn't leaving either. This was not the first time she'd done this and we were arguing. I knew she wouldn't call the cops—she was too full of crack herself. The dude that was with her came around the corner totally drunk on alcohol. He told me just to leave if I didn't want any trouble. Before he got the word "trouble" out his mouth, my left hand was in it and I punched him. He was wobbling trying to catch his balance. I grabbed him as if I was tackling him and ran him into the wrought iron gate in the fence as hard as I could. He let out a scream so scary, I just took off running. Amy called the police to my Uncle Craig's apartment where I stayed a lot when in Fountain Lakes.

I WENT TO JAIL THAT NIGHT.

My sister had an apartment in Jordan Cove in Dickinson near 517. She was hardly ever there so she let me go stay over there to keep me out of Texas City. It didn't help because I still went to Texas City every day because that's where the money was. I kept getting my court date reset trying to buy time, but I finally had to go on February 18, 2008. They asked me if I wanted to take my case to trial and I said yes, because I was thinking it might buy some more time. I was wrong. They told me to come back at one that afternoon to pick my jury. I really felt like I was railroaded, but that's what happens when you don't have a private lawyer.

On February 21, 2008 I was found guilty of possession of an unlawful firearm by a convicted felon and sentenced to five years in TDC, Texas Dept of Corrections. Oddly my jumpsuit had my name on the back of it—DOC—Dept of Corrections. It seemed like that was who I really was.

> *Thank God I have a new name now. It's still DOC, but it now stands for Disciple of Christ!*

BACK TO HOLIDAY FOR THE THIRD TIME

March 18, 2008 finds me walking through the back door of Holliday in Huntsville for the third time. I already know the ropes and the whole routine. I was there for five months and was sent to a private unit in Beaumont TX called Jefferson County Private Prison. It was cool over there—they had cell phones, weed, and cigarettes, not that they don't have them at every prison because they do, but this was wide open. I used to talk to my mom every night on the phone, and instead of my mom putting money on my books, I had a Hispanic homeboy that ran everything. My mom sent money through Moneygram to Z-man's wife. In exchange I got to use the phone and buy cigarettes and weed to sell. Even in jail I was hustling and I remember the K-9 Officer Horn told me at my trial that if nothing changes, then nothing changes.

THE PRODIGAL IN THE HOG BARN

I stayed in Beaumont for about five months and then was shipped to Eastham Trustee camp in Lovelady Texas, and that is where my life really changed. When I first got to that unit, I got to sit down and talk with the warden. He told me what will and will not happen on his unit. He also told me what will happen if I break any of those rules.
 Then they assign you a job. As we are talking the warden asked me if I was afraid of animals since I was a city boy. I was thinking of dogs, cats, cows, or horses. I said no so he put me in the HOG BARN! The next morning we got up for breakfast about 4:30 am. I ate and came to lie back down and dozed off when I heard banging on my cubicle. I opened my eyes and there was a guard shining a flashlight right in my face, an extra-bright light. He said, "Is your name Amey?" I said, "Yes sir." He said, "You didn't hear me calling your name?" It was time for work, so I got up to brush my teeth. He told me I had no time for that, and that I should have been up earlier. He called names in alphabetical order and mine was on the top of the list. If

he had to call my name again, I would be written up. We got on the bus—about 15 of us and they took us out to the hog barn. The first day I got off the bus; the smell was so awful, I lost my breakfast. A couple of the dudes started laughing and said "We got us a city boy here. Country boys are used to that smell but city boys can't handle it."

There was one big barn with about 20 sows, female pigs, in the middle. There were 15 males, boar hogs, on one side and 15 on the other. They had to separate the males. In the barn next to that, they kept the pregnant sows in cages till they were ready to give birth. They had some 30 young male boar hogs all in separate pens. Then there were rows and rows of female sows for breeding. My job was to spray out the big barn every day and feed the hogs. This went on for about six months, 7 days a week. I got used to it finally, but I hated it.

Doc Amey

CHAPTER 18

PAROLE COMES UP

It was a cold December day that I met the parole board, but I was denied. That meant I had to stay another whole year before I even got to come up for parole again. One cold December morning when I was spraying out the barn, I just stopped and looked up and said, "God, if You're real like everybody says You are, then You will get me out of this , and if You get me outta this then I'm through with the streets, the hustling, and everything!"

A crazy thing happened that day when I went back to the dorm, an older man that I only spoke to in passing, stopped me and asked me if I want to spread (meaning eat together) and talk because I looked like I had a lot on my mind. I was telling him how I hated working in the hog barn and how I just got denied by parole and how I wished I could get off this unit. He reminded me that by being a trustee all I had to do was put in for a trade that wasn't at our unit there. If I got accepted then they would have to ship me somewhere else that had that trade. He had a list of all the trades in TDC and he highlighted all the ones that were on our unit so I could avoid them. I filled out the request for about 20 different trades in TDC, and I ended up getting accepted to truck driving school on the Wynne Unit in Huntsville.

In January 2009 I got transferred to the Wynne Unit. It was totally opposite from Eastham because this unit was 95% black officers so I felt really at home in comparison. I got there a month before the truck driving school started so they had me working in the chicken yard, gathering eggs 7 days a week. In each house there were about 4,500 chickens, 5 or 6 to the cage. It was nothing I'd ever seen in my life. 75% of the chickens didn't even have feathers and were deathly skinny. Each chicken laid two eggs a day. We got there early in the morning and there were 3 people assigned to each house. First job we did was to pick up all the eggs and put them in egg crates, then we would get the rakes and clean all the chicken droppings from under the cages and spray the concrete in the middle walkway down. We then checked each cage to see if there were any wounded or dead chickens and pull them out.

By that time it would be lunch time and the boss would pick us up and take us back to camp to eat. After lunch he took us back to the chicken coop to do the same routine all over again.

I had hooked up with some brothers over there and started going to church. I got myself a Bible, started reading it and things began to look up, in fact they were looking great. I had no idea how great it was going to get.

In February of 2009 I began the six month course in truck driving class which I completed by August. We started going outside to actually practice in the truck, and they took us over to DPS to get our driver's permit so we can get out on the highway. When they ran my name, I found out my license had been suspended for six months starting that day. It was about the gun charges I had gotten. The suspension didn't go into effect until that day that I had applied for the permit. So, I had to sit around and wait for the six months to pass. I was a little discouraged seeing all the dudes I was in class with getting their permits, but I didn't let it get me down.

PAROLE COMES AROUND AGAIN--SEPTEMBER 8, 2009

I saw parole for the second time and my spirits were very high. I had been doing very well and feeling very good about it. Being on a trustee camp you weren't in a cell and there was no fence around the camp. As long as you weren't at work or class and it wasn't count time, you could roam freely throughout the camp. And on Fridays from 7 to 8 pm everyone who had seen parole could go to the Sergeant's office and they could check the computer to see if you got an answer—a yes or no to be let out. On average an answer takes between 60-90 days to hit the computer. I had just seen parole and it had only been a week. Some of the dudes I knew were going to check theirs and they said, "Hey look out Texas City, (that's what they called me), why not check the computer? You ain't got nothin' else to do." I said, "I doubt I have anything 'cause I just saw parole a week ago. They kept on, so I went and was third in line. The officer asked me my name and number and I replied "Amey—1489310." He typed it in and said, "FI-1". I was dumbfounded and said, "Are you sure?!" He typed it in again and said, "Yes, I'm sure—FI-1." The emotions I felt are unexplainable. An FI-1 is the best parole answer you can get and that means no classes required and no restrictions on me whatsoever. All I had to do was make sure I had somewhere to go and to verify it and I could go home! I was ecstatic. I walked out of there thanking God and praising Him for hearing my prayers. I wrote my mom that night and I got a letter two days later telling me that the parole people had called and everything was a go!

KEPT

Doc Amey

SECTION 3

I AM REDEEMED

CHAPTER 19

THE PRODIGAL GOES HOME

I got out of prison on November 23, 2009 with the joy of the Lord in my heart vowing never to step foot in a prison ever again except to preach or teach there. I caught the bus to Houston and guess what...My brother and his wife were there to get me. I've never in my life been so happy to see my brother and when I saw him, I prayed that God would take any hatred or other bad feelings out of my heart. This was just another sign that God was restoring my life to me when I thought it was over and done. God had plans for me.

My mom was living with her boyfriend, Mr. Phil. He told me I could use their address but I couldn't live there with them. So I moved in with my little sister in the Mainland Crossing Apts., sleeping on the couch.

I started going with my brother and his wife to a small Baptist Church in La,Marque. I didn't have a job so I had no money. I vowed never to sell or do drugs again, so I was totally dependent on others for a while. One day I was talking to the pastor's wife who also worked for the Financial Aid Dept at College of the Mainland. She talked to me about getting in school and learning a trade so I could get a good job. I did what she advised and got in the welding trade.

BACK CHILD SUPPORT

It was early 2010 and my sister and her boyfriend moved to a little 2 bedroom house/apartment on Westward and I still didn't have anywhere to live. She let me come and stay with her again. I walked to school every day then I went to a little job in the gym while I was in school. I was only making about 20 hours a week. It was not a full time job and I had kids to support. My kids' mother filed for benefits from the state and told them she didn't know where I was. Since I'd never had a job that I paid Social Security on, they never caught me. When I got that little part time job, they subpoenaed me to go to a hearing on the matter. They told me I'm in arrears to the state of Texas for $25,000. I owe the state $15,000 and I owe my children's mother $10,000 and if she was agreeable, she could drop her claim and I would only owe the state. She told them she is "not droppin' nothin'." So I've been trying to dig my way out of that hole ever since—and still digging!

CHAPTER 20

DETOURS

I moved in with a girl that I was seeing, and one night I heard her on the phone, crying. I ran up to see what was wrong. She was lying on the floor naked, talking incoherently and just tripping out. There was a knock on the door and it was the ambulance she had called. She had an aneurysm and they rushed her to the hospital. She was in a coma for about two weeks. Her mother turned into the devil and I didn't understand why. I found out this girl had had an accident in the refinery where she worked and there was a big settlement in the works that I was unaware of. When she came out of the coma, she kept asking about me because she didn't remember much.

Her mom started lying about me and just making things up. Her grandma was a God-fearing woman and I knew from the moment I met her that she was different. She told me that God had His hand on me and that she could see the anointing of God on my life. She was the only person taking my side against the lies being told. One day she told me I didn't need to go to the hospital for a while, just to let things cool off. I was hard-headed and went anyway. I was feeling a bit uneasy and one of "Sally's" (not her real name) friends was there. I kissed her and told her I'd be back later. As I went out there were four cops in the hall and I heard them talking, "The boyfriend is in there and he's not supposed to be." So I calmly walked right past them, got on the elevator and left. I couldn't stop thinking about what the grandma had said to me. It seemed God was in the process of closing some doors and opening others for my own good.

Let me say this, no matter what I have ever been going through, my mother always had my back. Even the three trips to prison, she was the only one in my corner. My mother and I are born exactly one week apart, so we have always shared a special bond. To this day my mother is my best friend, whom I love very dearly.

I moved back in with my mother, who now had an apartment in Mainland Crossing. I was still going to welding school, and still going to church. In the summer of 2011 the church planned a trip to Orlando FL to see the Holy Land Experience. It's a big theme park that's built to look like Jerusalem. I was so excited to go, and it was so awesome. However, some things that happened I didn't understand as a new Christian. I just stopped going to church after that and started smoking weed and drinking again. Another detour on the way to where God wanted me to be.

GETTING ON MY FEET

I got a job at Bebco Industries as a welder. I worked for a month then the child support kicked in and deducted half my paycheck. I want to support my kids but I needed to live too. When I was able to get financial aid, I paid for my classes, my books, welding equipment and still had money left over. I had my mind set on getting a Buick LeSabre. I didn't care what year it was, I just knew that's what I wanted. Everywhere I went to look they wanted $2000-

$3000 down and that didn't include any payments. I ended up getting a 1991 Honda Accord for $750 cash and I spent about that much more doing some work on it.

PASTOR KEVIN

In the fall of 2011, I was at my son's football game and I noticed a white guy to my right about 30 feet over. He kept staring at me and I was starting to feel uncomfortable. He looks very familiar but I couldn't quite place him. I keep asking myself "Where do I know him from?" I'm not the type to steal or rob and he doesn't look like he's on drugs, so it's not adding up. I was thinking, when halftime came around I was going to go over and find out who he is. When the whistle blew, I made a beeline toward him and all of a sudden with this big smile I could never forget, he said, "Doc Amey! " It was really loud, and when I heard his voice it all came back to me. I knew exactly who he was. He was Brother Kevin Herrin from Christ Temple on 29th Street where I attended Sunday School back when I was a kid! We talked and hugged and it had been about 21 years since we had seen each other. The Rawls kids were still going to his church all those years, so he kept up with where I was. He told me they had a new church on 146, The Fellowship and that he was now the Senior Pastor. He invited me to come and I told him I would. We went our separate ways, but obviously God was giving me a path to follow that would keep me from the next episode in my journey. I again made the wrong decision.

Doc Amey

CHAPTER 21

BACK IN THE GAME

The enemy came knocking on my door October 21, 2011. My uncle passed away and my cousin from California called and told me his dad didn't have any insurance and that he was in Texas City. He said he had some drugs to sell—some "drank" syrup and "Dro", hydro weed. He said I didn't have to touch any of it, would I just connect him to some of my old customers? This was one of my favorite cousins so without thinking twice I said yes. I was helping him get the stuff sold, doing a good deed for my family, right? The whole time I was giving people my number. About a week later he called and told me that his plane leaves in an hour and would I take what he had left and sell for him.

Sadly, though my intentions were good, trying to help him, I was back in the game, "ten toes down" smoking weed, sipping "drank", and back hustling. I was also working on my welding job, so I hadn't completely let go of my new life. I had one foot on the pier and the other one in the boat, so to speak. Soon I would have to make a decision on which way to jump.

In December 2011, I was on a train heading to CA to pick up a very large shipment of drugs, just in time for Christmas. I got it and was told how I was going to make all this money because I had two suitcases full of drugs. I made it back to San Antonio to the train station. My cousin called and told me his brother-in-law was picking me up and driving me to Houston. I was okay with that.

We got to Houston okay, but to my surprise, my CA cousin was there waiting for me. I started thinking of what was going on and figured out that I'd been used like a pawn in a chess game. Red flags were flying in my head because I was still on parole! If I was caught, I'd be out of there! He allowed me a small fraction of what was in the cases and said, "Here this is for you and you don't owe me nothing, but from now on, I'm gonna need money up front!" It was a total betrayal and a slap in the face that I'd been played that bad. I would not deal with him again.

Instead of seeing this as a sign I was on the wrong track, I got myself another connection on the weed, my "potna Smack", and for the "drank" syrup I started dealing with another cousin here.

A WORD FROM GOD

One day I was searching in my closet for something and a box fell out on the floor. I know I did nothing to cause it to fall. It must have been another sign from God. I picked it up and saw it was all my papers from prison—letters, parole certificate, pictures, etc. I distinctly heard God say clear as day, "What are you doing?" "I thought you said IF I would get you out of that prison I wouldn't have to worry about you. WHAT ARE YOU DOING?!"

I was tripping! I had to stop this! I immediately called Everick Rawls, my neighbor that I went to church with as a kid, and asked him what time the services started at The Fellowship. He told me 9am and 11am and I said, "Man, I gotta get back in church. Even then I procrastinated a few more weeks. I got off parole December 29, 2012.

KEPT

Doc Amey

CHAPTER 22

FINALLY HOME

One Sunday morning the girl I was with and I got dressed and went to church. Pastor Kevin wasn't there that morning because he'd gone to New York City to visit his daughter who lived there. It was August so school had just started back. The first person I ran into was Brother Bud who used to twist my ear and demand that I be good in service. The first words out of his mouth were, "Well, look what the wind blew in!" From the second I stepped a foot in that church I felt a peace come over my body and mind, and I knew I was finally home.

STARTING THE BUS MINISTRY

I began going to church faithfully every Sunday and Wednesday and it wasn't long before I was volunteering to help park cars. Every Sunday I came to church I would see the red van parked there in the back and never moving.

I asked Pastor Kevin why there was no bus ministry for the church. He said, "I have the bus, and a driver but I don't have any kids." I said, "Okay, that's MY job because I know where to get the kids. I was brought to church when I was a kid so I have to bring some too." It was and is so important in my life to help these kids and expose them to the Lord Jesus Christ, who died for them and wants to provide a good life and perfect peace in this troubled world. I started the bus ministry at the church, going out and gathering the kids and now I'm the driver!

Going to church even for a short time creates a compass point in their lives that will show them the way "home" even when they are as lost as I was for many years.

THE SATURDAY PRAYER GROUP & TERRY MELANCON

I got more and more committed to The Fellowship and started faithfully attending the Saturday morning prayer group with some of the elders. God led me to a wonderful mentor, a man named Terry Melancon. He has been an incredible influence in my life of how a young black man should stand up and be mature. I didn't have a father's influence growing up but now I have that in him and many others.

One Saturday morning, he wasn't at the prayer meeting, so I stopped by his house afterwards to check on him and make sure he was okay. As I was driving down his street, I saw him mowing his lawn, so I knew he was okay. It was around 11:30 that he finished mowing. We talked for a bit and went into the house and I sat down on the couch and we watched the pre-game of the Final Four in college basketball. We talked about the teams that were playing and who we thought would win.

Terry and I had on several occasions talked about our love for crawfish, but had never had a chance to cook any. His wife called home and he told her I was there, but the call was short and nothing else was said. About 45 minutes later Terry's wife arrived home with ten pounds of live crawfish and all the trimmings! She had seasoning, corn, potatoes and sausage. To this day Terry will not admit that he told his wife to bring the crawfish, but I know he did. We boiled the crawfish and watched the Final Four. I left around nine that night.

I read some scriptures that night before I went to bed that changed my life from that day: Col. 4:7-8 "7-Tychicus, a beloved brother, faithful minister and fellow servant in the Lord will tell you all the news about me. 8-I am sending him to you for this very purpose, that he may know your circumstances and comfort your heart."

That was a Rhema (a word which means God speaking right now) word to me and I called Mr. Terry and told him God had shown me that he was meant to be in my life as a mentor. He asked me why I thought that so I read the scripture to him and changed the name to Mr. Terry in the place of Tychicus. It was confirmed by the Holy Spirit right then and there. He began mentoring me one on one.

We have had some good times at the Rockets game and Mega-Fest in Dallas where we spent three intense days of digging into the Word, and we're still going strong having Bible studies almost every morning while I was unemployed. His words have always been the same—"Trust God", and my favorite, "Well, Doc, what does the Bible say?" He has been an incredible spiritual father to me and has shown me in deed, not just in words, what a real man of God looks like. I thank God for Terry Melancon!

THE BUICK LESABRE

One Saturday morning, I saw a woman pull up in a white Buick LeSabre and when she walked in the church I said, "Ma'am, (I didn't know her name then), if you ever decide to sell that car, please give me first dibbs to buy it from you, because I love that car." It was about February or March when this happened. I was going to church faithfully, reading my Bible, working my job, and staying clean. My little Honda started breaking down, but I kept believing God and keeping the faith. I was baptized in water in February of 2013 and baptized in the Holy Spirit with the evidence of speaking in tongues right around the same time.

One day, after church, I was reading my Bible and this scripture came alive to me:

> "And by their prayers for you, who long for you because of the exceeding grace of God in you, Thanks be to God for His indescribable gift.",II Corinthians 9:14-15, NKJ

That was a powerful or Rhema word for me. I felt it deep down in my spirit that God was about to do something big for me. I ran into my mom's room and read her the verses I'd gotten.

Her first response was "Go buy a lottery ticket!" For the next couple of weeks I bought lotto tickets. I know, right? But one day April 5, 2013 to be exact, it was on a Friday because Mr. Terry and I were used to having breakfast every Friday at Denny's. We were sitting there talking and waiting on our food and my phone rang. I was looking at the phone and it was a number I didn't know. I don't usually answer the phone when I don't know who it is, but the Holy Spirit said, "Answer the phone!" I answered and the woman on the other end said, "Hello I'd like to speak to Doc." I said, "This is him." She said, "This is Mrs Luanne, white Buick LeSabre. " I said, "Oh, hey Mrs Luanne. How you doin'?" She said, "Just fine. I'm calling because God told me to give you this car I said "what car" she said "this white Buick LeSabre you love so much!" I was really caught off guard and like man, is this some kind of a joke? Where I come from people don't just give other people cars! She said, "No, it's not a joke. God told me to give this car to you, and if you want to meet me somewhere we can go down to the DMV and get the title switched over ." Still in shock, I said, "Yeah, I'm eating right now but I will call you soon as I finish." She said, "Okay, I am waiting on your call."

When I hung up I told Mr. Terry what happened and said, "I'm not even hungry no more." Right when I was about to cancel my order, the waiter came with the food. I took about two bites and told Mr. Terry I was too excited to eat. I got a to-go box and called Ms. Luanne back and she met me at the church. We got in the car and she told me, "I knew I was going to give you that car from the second you asked me about it! My husband and I got that car two years ago when my mother in law went to be with the Lord, and we were just waiting until the Lord led us to give it to someone." When we got to the DMV to transfer the title, she paid for the transfer! She said, "It's a gift and I don't want it to come out of your pocket or cost you anything." This was the indescribable gift that I read about in II Corinthians 9! How do you describe that feeling of being so blessed?

There is always someone who questions God's blessing. One dude went as far as saying that I had to be sleeping with the older women in the church because "don't nobody just give you no car". I said I might have thought that too before I knew the Lord. My God is generous!

MY NEW FRONT TEETH

As you may recall, I had an incident with my teeth earlier in my life. Well, about a month after my initial visit to Bible College, Pastor Kevin's mother, Pastor Eloise, set me up to see a dentist and find out what could be done to get me some front teeth. The church paid for X-rays and an exam at the Crown Dental next to Kroger. They gave me an estimate of close to $5000. I told them that I would like to get a second opinion and really I just didn't have faith anyone could pay that much for me. I sure didn't have that much money.

Pastor Eloise was talking to a young lady in our church about this, and she happened to work for a dentist here in Texas City. She said ,"Let me tell Dr. Brandon Fleshman about this situation and just see if he offers any assistance. He's a very generous person and who knows? "
  She mentioned me to him and Pastor Eloise talked to him but neither asked him to do any work. They thought they could maybe raise the money to cover it, if I could get an idea of the cost. He told them to make me an appointment and he would see what had to be done. I went in and the Dr. did the whole exam on me. He told me I needed a few teeth pulled, a few root canals, some fillings, and some other things, mainly a bridge to replace

my missing teeth in front. My mouth was really jacked up. I've never had insurance of any kind, and the only time I ever saw a doctor was in an emergency. He told me all that I needed done then asked me if I was ready to get started with the procedures. I said let me call Pastor Eloise and ask her what she wants me to do. He said, "She has nothing to do with this—it's up to you." I was floored. He did everything he named to me FREE of charge! I can't tell you how happy I was. For the first time in 17 years I wasn't ashamed to smile! So if you see me smiling just remember I have 17 years of smiling to make up for. God had once again fulfilled II Cor. 9 with an indescribable gift!

STARTING FELLOWSHIP BIBLE COLLEGE

Mr. Terry invited me to come and sit in one of his classes at the Fellowship Bible School so I went on a Monday night for the first time. When I walked in a lady came to me and said, "Hello, my name is Gina Estey and I'm the Bible College Director. I'm not just saying this because you're standing here in front of me." She called her husband over and said, "Tell him, Chuck. I told my husband yesterday when I noticed you in praise and worship. God's got His hand on that young man. We need to get him in Bible School." She invited me to sit in the last eight weeks of that spring semester. I enrolled in Fellowship Bible College in the fall of 2013.

KIDS CAMP—JUNE 2013 & 2014

Our church has four camps for kids and youth that is intense praise, study, play, and learning. I got to go to the Kids Camp and stay as a chaperone. I will never forget that experience. My dorm was mostly kids with special needs and by the end of the week, I had bonded with those kids like I could never have imagined. In 2014, I went to camp again. I can't wait to go again this summer. It's truly the highlight of the year for all our kids, but especially for some of my bus kids that have never been anywhere and their lives are forever changed and blessed.

MY VERY OWN APARTMENT

I did something I'd never done before—got my very own apartment. Even though it was in my mom's name, it was mine. My mom signed the lease for me because I couldn't get one due to my felonies. I have a mountain of child support and back child support so it is difficult seeing only half my paycheck to pay my bills. I committed to paying my tithes when I first got into the Fellowship. I didn't understand it at first, but the Lord proved that he would bless me and stretch my money, just like it says in Malachi 3.

MY CHRISTMAS MIRACLE 2014

Paying for my own place and all my bills has been a struggle, but God has helped me. I have four kids and Christmas was coming and I was stressing and worrying about how I would do anything for them. I was at Buccee's discussing this with the mother of one of my children. Then suddenly a woman who was filling her tank with gas on the other side of the pump overheard our conversation and she walked over and said to me, "God said don't worry. He's got your back!" She walked away and I felt instant peace in my spirit. Christmas was on a Thursday and the Sunday before Christmas I was at the door at church, greeting the people as I always do every Sunday. One of the ushers walked up to me, handed me an envelope, and said the person that gave me this for you asked me not to reveal who it was, but said Merry Christmas. I felt the envelope and it feels thick and heavy, so I was very curious. I went to the red bus we use to pick up kids or take them home and opened the envelope. It was $500 in twenties! Talk about "in the nick of time!" We had an awesome Christmas. God again brought II Cor. 9 back to mind. When God makes a promise, He always keeps His Word if we just believe Him and trust in Him!

THE NEW YEAR WITH NEW BLESSINGS 2015

January 2015 came in with new hope for greater things. I was laid off from my job that I had worked on for three years. It's difficult to find work because most people don't care that you've totally turned your life around, all they see is what's on paper. I am believing God for my future and I know that He will take care of me.

March 25 began a five service revival meeting with Luke Holter. The final service on Wednesday night, I received a word of prophecy from the Lord that I should write a book of my personal testimony. I was to tell of my brokenness and my life of poverty and drugs and trouble—everything God has saved me from and everything He has done for me. He said God would breathe the breath of life into it, and it would bless people around the globe. I know that the blessing is right on the other side of obedience, so here you have it, my life story, raw and uncut. I pray you are touched by it and that it blesses you and helps you to avoid the same mistakes I made. Every account is real with real dates and mostly real names, though some have been changed to protect the guilty. Some are not given because they are still in the game (business of dealing drugs). My story is not even close to being finished. It is still being written, but I know God will always cause me to triumph and my life will be a fragrant aroma of Christ to those who need Him so desperately. II Cor. 2:14,15

FINISHING FELLOWSHIP BIBLE COLLEGE

I just graduated with an Associate Degree in Religious Studies in May of 2015. I haven't missed a single class and I have straight A's! Only God could change me, from the way I used to be! (II Cor. 9 again!)

Fellowship Bible College
Est. 2011

On recommendation of the faculty and directors, the President and Pastor of Fellowship Bible College has conferred on

Edward "Doc" Amey

the degree of

Associate of Biblical Studies

and has granted this Diploma as evidence thereof, given at Texas City, Texas this twenty-seventh day of May, 2015

Dean of Students

Pastor, President

Fellowship

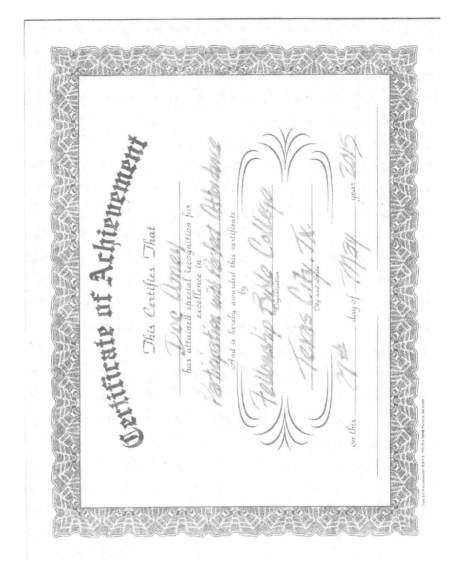

On one of the last nights of school, one of my Bible Instructors Pastor Jimmy Kirby spoke a word over me. He said God would open doors for me to bring Jesus to all the nations.

Trusting in the word from God, I tried to get my passport so I would be ready. I found out that because of back child support I would not be allowed to get one. I found out that God is bigger than any government documentation!

REPPIN' JESUS CHRIST TO THE WORLD

Remember Officer Sal Chapa, the one who called me Cinderella and arrested me on a gun charge, sending me to prison for the third (and last) time?

I was at a community cook off and Officer Chapa was there. It was during a time of unrest between officers and young black males. I sensed the Holy Spirit speak to me and tell me to pray for Officer Chapa and his safety. We went around the side of the building for privacy, but unknowingly, at the time, someone snapped a photo of the two of us holding hands and praying together. They posted the image on social media and it went viral!

We became the face of unity and reconciliation to not only viewers in the United States, but also across the world. God used me to represent Jesus across the world and I never left Texas City!

Photo credit Kevin Woods

I encourage everyone to work towards unity. The issues in our country is not a skin issue---they are a sin issue.

Big things happened from there!

God opened the door for my story to be featured in Crossroads Bible Institute's Newsletter.

Finding God in a Pigsty

"Denied parole and in the first year of a five year prison sentence, Edward Amey was at a low point in his life. When he was not in his cell, he was working in the prison's hog barn, feeding and cleaning up after pigs. Ashamed by his past and frustrated by his present situation, Amey cried out to the God he once knew in his childhood. "God, if you're really real, like everyone says, will you get me out of here? If I get out, I'm through. I'm through with the drugs and the women. I will surrender my life to you," he prayed. **** When Amey was born in Galveston, Texas, in 1980, his father nicknamed him Doc. He still isn't sure why he was given the name, but somehow it stuck. Six months and nine days after Amey was born, his father died. His mother was an addict, crack her drug of choice. Many of his family members were also in the drug game, and Amey struggled to find a father figure. "My mom was on crack, my brother was selling drugs, my uncle was using drugs. Nothing but drugs everywhere around me," Amey said. "It was rough as a child." Eventually, Amey's mother got clean for a while when Amey was ten years old, and they started going to church. The children's pastor made an impact on his young life. "That church made an impression on me. They made me realize no matter how far I went, I could return to God," Amey said. "That was one of the happiest times of my life." But after his family moved to a rough neighborhood in Texas City, Amey got caught up in selling and using drugs and wandered off from God. "At age eleven, I started smoking weed, having sex and running the streets. I started selling drugs at age fourteen. By the age of seventeen, I had two women pregnant," he said. "I was living life the way I thought it was supposed to be lived." Soon Amey found himself getting in trouble with the law. He landed in jail and prison several times, mostly on drug charges. Every time he was released, he returned to his life of crime. "When I would get out, I'd do the same thing. Partying, doing drugs, selling drugs, drinking," Amey said. In December 2006, Amey was high and in possession of drugs and a handgun when he saw several police cars in a parking lot. When one of the officers confronted Amey, he took off running. Amey thought he had eluded police when he got inside a friend's house. But he was caught when officers came to the home looking for another suspect. After his conviction, Amey found himself in prison for a third time on a five year sentence. It was during this stint that he found himself working in the pigsty, desperately calling out to God to deliver him from his situation "God, if you're really real, like everyone says, will you get me out of here?" After that prayer, Amey sensed God's presence and began seeking Him. He enrolled with Crossroad Bible Institute, flying through the Great Truths of the Bible course in less than a year. Amey said the lessons kept him grounded during difficult times and pointed him to encouragement and wisdom from Scripture. "It gave me a program to go by. I didn't have to find my own way while reading the Bible. I didn't have to blindly open my Bible and try to figure stuff out on my own," Amey said. Within months of finishing the Great Truths of the Bible course, Amey's prayer was answered. He was paroled early for good behavior in 2009. "I was on fire for God, man. I started going to church, and I was doing good," Amey said. But in 2011, his uncle died, and his cousin was short on money for the funeral. In order to help his cousin with expenses after the death of his father,

Amey stepped back into the drug game. "I thought I was just doing my family a favor. The devil had me blind," Amey said. "Soon I'm back to selling and doing drugs, back to everything I told God I wouldn't do." But God didn't stop pursuing him. One day when Amey was going through his closet, he had what he calls a "God moment." A box fell off a shelf in the closet. It was filled with items from his time in prison—letters, forms, parole certificates and CBI materials. Amey was reminded of his promise to the Lord while he was behind bars. "I heard the Holy Spirit saying, 'What are you doing? I thought you were going to follow me,'" Amey said. "I realized I can't walk with God and still dance with the devil." Just days before that encounter with the Lord, Amey had run into his former children's pastor, who now is a senior pastor and had invited Amey to his church. He began attending the church but had "one leg in the church and the other leg in the world," Amey said. "Slowly but surely God made Himself clear to me, and I began to change," Amey said. He cut off all ties to his former life of drugs and crime. He volunteered for his church's bus ministry and studied at a Bible college, earning an associate's degree. Amey has also had it on his heart to pray for police officers. Last year, someone spotted him praying for a Texas City cop. A photo of the encounter was posted on Facebook and soon went viral. The story was picked up by several national media outlets. "That officer was the same one who had arrested me on the gun charge. God set it up," Amey said. Reflecting on his past, Amey said he is thankful for God's redemptive work in his life. "Looking back at my old life shows me how lost I really was and how lost my people are," he said, rattling off some of his six felonies and more than twenty misdemeanors. He said he regrets his past life of crime but recognizes that God is using his past to minister to others. "I wouldn't be reaching the people that I am reaching now if I hadn't gone through it," he said. In light of his transformation, Amey's nickname has now taken on new meaning.

"I'm Doc—Disciple of Christ," he said.

Written by Aaron Mueller, communications director of Crossroad Bible Institute

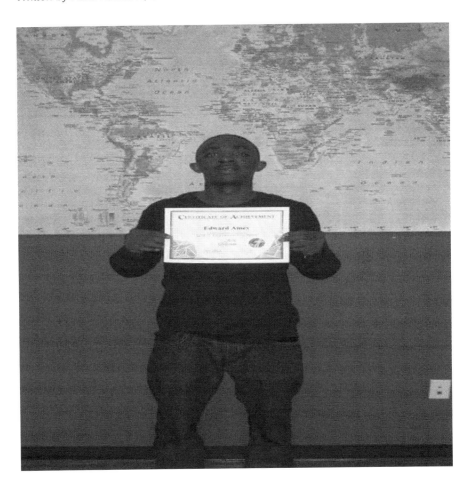

PIT TO THE PALACE

Magic doesn't only happen for Cinderella. The following picture is of me and the Galveston County District Attorney, Jack Roady.

Jack Roady and I met at the celebration party for the now Galveston County Commissioner, Darrell Apffel. Unknown to me before this meeting, Mr. Roady had been following me on Facebook since the media explosion after I prayed for Officer Chapa. The night Mr. Roady and I met, I found out that he had prosecuted some of my cases as had been inspired by how God had intervened and changed my life.

Mr. Roady invited me to the Pregnancy and Parenting Fundraiser and we took this picture together at that event. Who would have thought me, Doc Amey, 6 time felon, and having been to prison 3 times, would be sharing meals with the same guy who prosecuted some of my cases in the past. ONLY GOD!!!

Image taken by Chris Bell

I know this isn't the end of my story. I am excited to see what miraculous thing He has in store next. So stay tuned and God's miracles and mercies never cease!

I pray that I am touching lives around my city especially, because many knew me back then and how I used to be, and the difference now is evident in my life. Thank you for taking the time to read my book and if you know someone this might bless and inspire, please share with them.

Doc Amey

> D. O. C. was Department of Corrections
>
> Now
>
> D. O. C. Disciple of Christ

If you would like to contact Doc about bringing his message of being Kept to your organization, or if you would like to support his message and help it reach others with the hope of Christ, please contact him.

Lostandfoundministry2016@gmail.com

www.sowtolostandfoundministry.com

ABOUT THE AUTHOR

Doc Amey is a father of 4, that grew up born and raised in Texas City, Texas. He graduated bible college as Salutatorians with perfect attendance. He founded Lost & Found Ministries and goes in to prisons and detention centers ministering and giving hope to the lost with his message of how God Kept him and is still keeping him.

Made in the USA
San Bernardino, CA
30 July 2018